studysync®

Reading & Writing Companion
American Literature

UNIT 5

:: studysync®

studysync.com

ISBN 978-1-97-016216-5

4 5 6 7 8 SKY 26 25 24 23 22

C

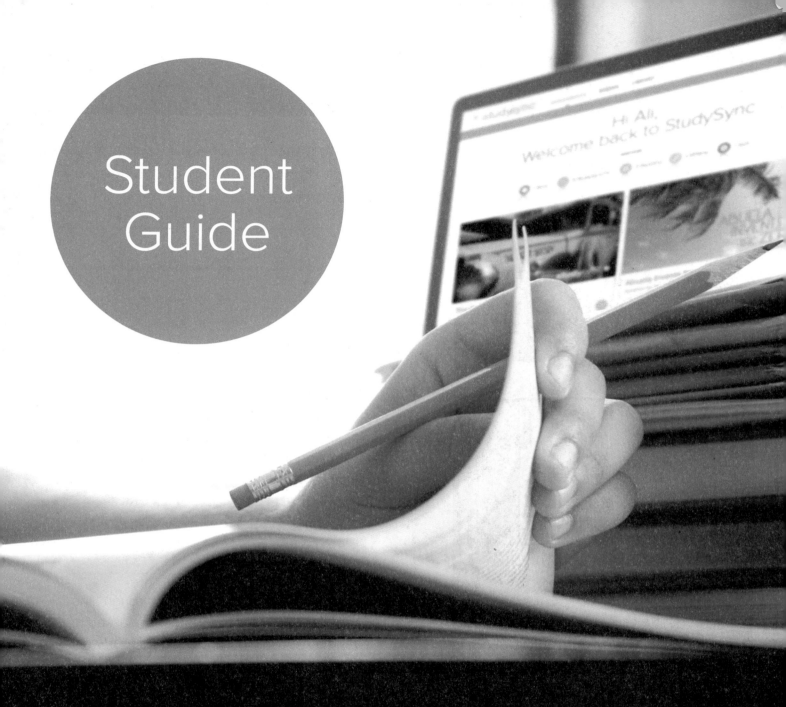

Student Guide

Getting Started

Welcome to the StudySync Reading & Writing Companion! In this book, you will find a collection of readings based on the literary focus of the unit you are studying. As you work through the readings, you will be asked to answer questions and perform a variety of tasks designed to help you closely analyze and understand each text selection. Read on for an explanation of each section of this book.

Close Reading and Writing Routine

In each unit, you will read texts and text excerpts that are from or are in some way connected to a particular period of American literature. Each reading encourages a closer look through questions and a short writing assignment.

① Introduction

An Introduction to each text provides historical context for your reading as well as information about the author. You will also learn about the genre of the text and the year in which it was written.

② Notes

Many times, while working through the activities after each text, you will be asked to **annotate** or **make annotations** about what you are reading. This means that you should highlight or underline words in the text and use the "Notes" column to make comments or jot down any questions you have. You may also want to note any unfamiliar vocabulary words here.

You will also see sample student annotations to go along with the Skill lesson for that text.

3 First Read

During your first reading of each selection, you should just try to get a general idea of the content and message of the reading. Don't worry if there are parts you don't understand or words that are unfamiliar to you. You'll have an opportunity later to dive deeper into the text.

4 Think Questions

These questions will ask you to start thinking critically about the text, asking specific questions about its purpose, and making connections to your prior knowledge and reading experiences. To answer these questions, you should go back to the text and draw upon specific evidence to support your responses. You will also begin to explore some of the more challenging vocabulary words in the selection.

5 Skills

Each Skill includes two parts: Checklist and Your Turn. In the Checklist, you will learn the process for analyzing the text. The model student annotations in the text provide examples of how you might make your own notes following the instructions in the Checklist. In the Your Turn, you will use those same instructions to practice the skill.

---

3  First Read

Read the Constitution of the Iroquois Nations. After you read, complete the Think Questions below.

4 ☁ THINK QUESTIONS

1. Do you think that the "Tree of the Great Peace" is real, symbolic, or a combination of both? Support your interpretation with evidence from the text.

2. According to Articles 1 and 10, how did the role of the Onondaga people differ from the roles of the other four tribes of the Iroquois nation? Provide details from the text to support your answer.

3. What does the bundle of arrows in Article 57 symbolize? What does this symbolism suggest is the main purpose of the Iroquois Constitution? Provide details from the text to support your answer.

4. Consider the usage of the word **unanimously** within the text in Article 10. Do you think that the initial letters *un* in *unanimously* refer to the Latin prefix for "one" (as in *unicycle*) or "not" (as in *uncooperative*)? Use evidence from the text to support your answer.

5. Use context to determine the meaning of the word **upbraid** as it is used in the Constitution of the Iroquois Nations. Write your definition of *upbraid* here and explain which context clues helped you determine its meaning.

---

5  Skill: Central or Main Idea

Use the Checklist to analyze Central or Main Idea in the Constitution of the Iroquois Nations. Refer to the sample student annotations about Central or Main Ideas in the text.

••• CHECKLIST FOR CENTRAL OR MAIN IDEA

In order to identify two or more central ideas of a text, note the following:

✓ the main idea in each paragraph or group of paragraphs

✓ key details in each paragraph or section of text, distinguishing what they have in common

✓ whether the details contain information that could indicate more than one main idea in a text

   • a science text, for example, may provide information about a specific environment and also a message on ecological awareness

   • a biography may contain equally important ideas about a person's achievements, influence, and the time period in which the person lives or lived

✓ when each central idea emerges

✓ ways that the central ideas interact and build on one another

To determine two or more central ideas of a text and analyze their development over the course of the text, including how they interact and build on one another to provide a complex analysis, consider the following questions:

✓ What main idea(s) do the details in each paragraph explain or describe?

✓ What central or main ideas do all the paragraphs support?

✓ How do the central ideas interact and build on one another? How does that affect when they emerge?

✓ How might you provide an objective summary of the text? What details would you include?

♺ YOUR TURN

1. This question has two parts. First, answer Part A. Then, answer Part B.

Part A: Which of the following central tenets or beliefs of the Five Nations can be inferred from this passage?

- ○ A. Women had all the political power.
- ○ B. Women decided who could be leaders.
- ○ C. Men had all the political power.
- ○ D. Men decided who could be leaders.

Part B: Which excerpt from the passage best provides evidence to support the answer identified in Part A?

- ○ A. "If a Lord of the Confederacy should seek to establish any authority independent of the jurisdiction of the Confederacy of the Great Peace, which is the Five Nations . . ."
- ○ B. ". . . he shall be warned three times in open council, first by the women relatives . . ."
- ○ C. "If the offending Lord is still obdurate he shall be dismissed by the War Chief . . ."
- ○ D. "His nation shall then install the candidate nominated by the female name holders of his family."

6

NOTES

Skill:
Central or Main
Idea

This paragraph
discusses the details of
how decisions are made
within the tribes. I
wonder if these details
support a main idea
that the tribes
established procedures
to make decisions even
when there was
disagreement . . . .

10. In all cases the procedure must be as follows: when the Mohawk and Seneca Lords have **unanimously** agreed upon a question, they shall report their decision to the Cayuga and Oneida Lords who shall deliberate upon the question and report a unanimous decision to the Mohawk Lords. The Mohawk Lords will then report the standing of the case to the Firekeepers, who shall **render** a decision as they see fit in case of a disagreement by the two bodies, or confirm the decisions of the two bodies if they are identical. The Fire Keepers shall then report their decision to the Mohawk Lords who shall announce it to the open council.

11. If through any misunderstanding or obstinacy on the part of the Fire Keepers, they render a decision at variance with that of the Two Sides, the Two Sides shall reconsider the matter and if their decisions are jointly the same as before they shall report to the Fire Keepers who are then compelled to confirm their joint decision.

...

Rights, Duties and Qualifications of Lords

...

19. If at any time it shall be manifest that a Confederate Lord has not in mind the welfare of the people or disobeys the rules of this Great Law, the men or women of the Confederacy, or both jointly, shall come to the Council and **upbraid** the erring Lord through his War Chief. If the complaint of the people through the War Chief is not heeded the first time it shall be uttered again and then if no attention is given a third complaint and warning shall be given. If the Lord is contumacious the matter shall go to the council of War Chiefs. The War Chiefs shall then divest the erring Lord of his title by order of the women in whom the titleship is vested. When the Lord is deposed the women shall notify the Confederate Lords through their War Chief, and the Confederate Lords shall sanction the act. The women will then select another of their sons as a candidate and the Lords shall elect him. Then shall the chosen one be installed by the Installation Ceremony.

When a Lord is to be deposed, his War Chief shall address him as follows:

"So you, _____, disregard and set at naught the warnings of your women relatives. So you fling the warnings over your shoulder to cast them behind you.

"Behold the brightness of the Sun and in the brightness of the Sun's light I depose you of your title and remove the sacred emblem of your Lordship

---

Close Read

6

Reread the Constitution of the Iroquois Nations. As you reread, complete the Skills Focus questions below. Then use your answers and annotations from the questions to help you complete the Write activity.

 SKILLS FOCUS

1. Explain how the word *binding* relates to one of the main ideas of the Constitution of the Iroquois Nations, citing specific examples from the document to support your response.

2. Identify and summarize important leadership qualities in the Confederacy and explain how the ideas about leadership interact with and build on another main idea in the articles.

3. Explain how sections of the Constitution of the Iroquois Nations remind you of ideas that would eventually shape the early American identity, citing specific evidence from the text to support your response.

WRITE

EXPLANATORY: Most historians believe the Constitution of the Iroquois Nations inspired the framers of the U.S. Constitution. Write a response that explains the similarities between the main ideas of the Constitution of the Iroquois Nations and the principles you believe are relevant in America today. Use evidence from the text and your own experiences to support your response.

7

6

Close Read & Skills Focus

After you have completed the First Read, you will be asked to go back and read the text more closely and critically. Before you begin your Close Read, you should read through the Skills Focus to get an idea of the concepts you will want to focus on during your second reading. You should work through the Skills Focus by making annotations, highlighting important concepts, and writing notes or questions in the "Notes" column. Depending on instructions from your teacher, you may need to respond online or use a separate piece of paper to start expanding on your thoughts and ideas.

7

Write

Your study of each selection will end with a writing assignment. For this assignment, you should use your notes, annotations, personal ideas, and answers to both the Think and the Skills Focus questions. Be sure to read the prompt carefully and address each part of it in your writing.

Extended Writing Project and Grammar

This is your opportunity to use genre characteristics and craft to compose meaningful, longer written works exploring the theme of each unit. You will draw information from your readings, research, and own life experiences to complete the assignment.

1 Writing Project

After you have read all of the unit text selections, you will move on to a writing project. Each project will guide you through the process of writing your essay. Student models will provide guidance and help you organize your thoughts. One unit ends with an **Extended Oral Project,** which will give you an opportunity to develop your oral language and communication skills.

2 Writing Process Steps

There are four steps in the writing process: Plan, Draft, Revise, and Edit and Publish. During each step, you will form and shape your writing project, and each lesson's peer review will give you the chance to receive feedback from your peers and teacher.

3 Writing Skills

Each Skill lesson focuses on a specific strategy or technique that you will use during your writing project. Each lesson presents a process for applying the skill to your own work and gives you the opportunity to practice it to improve your writing.

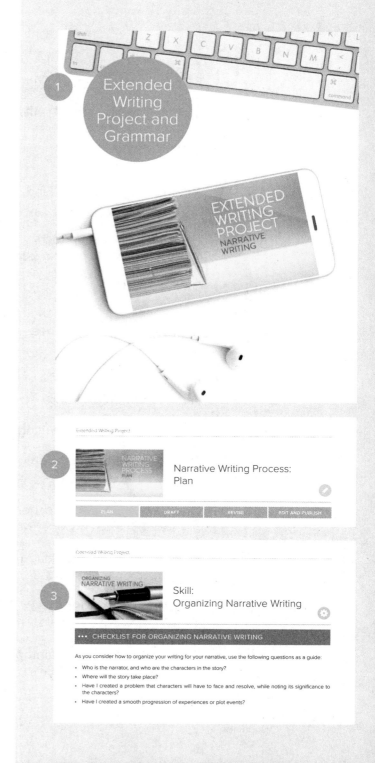

Life, Liberty, and the Pursuit of Happiness

How do our goals inform our actions?

Literary Focus: THE POSTWAR AND CIVIL RIGHTS ERAS

Texts

 Paired Readings

Extended Writing Project and Grammar

Talk Back Texts are works from a later period that engage with the themes and tropes of the unit's literary focus. Demonstrating that literature is always in conversation, these texts provide dynamic new perspectives to complement the unit's more traditional chronology.

Please note that excerpts and passages in the StudySync® library and this workbook are intended as touchstones to generate interest in an author's work. The excerpts and passages do not substitute for the reading of entire texts, and StudySync® strongly recommends that students seek out and purchase the whole literary or informational work in order to experience it as the author intended. Links to online resellers are available in our digital library. In addition, complete works may be ordered through an authorized reseller by filling out and returning to StudySync® the order form enclosed in this workbook.

Reading & Writing Companion   **ix**

How do our goals inform our actions?

LORRAINE HANSBERRY

Lorraine Hansberry (1930–1965) was born in the South Side of Chicago to a prominent African American family that called W. E. B. Du Bois, Langston Hughes, and Duke Ellington friends. Her father had founded one of Chicago's first banks for African Americans, yet the family faced opposition and violence when they bought a new home. Her family's experience with discrimination led to a case that ultimately went to the Supreme Court.

JOHN HERSEY

Born to American missionary parents in Tianjin, China, John Hersey (1914–1993) spoke Chinese before learning English. After moving to the United States at the age of ten, Hersey attended Yale University where he played football and was coached by Gerald Ford, the future president. As a journalist, Hersey pioneered what became known as New Journalism, a style of writing that uses the storytelling techniques of fiction to relate nonfiction events. This technique was later adopted by twentieth-century writers such as Truman Capote and Norman Mailer.

LANGSTON HUGHES

A leader of the Harlem Renaissance, Langston Hughes (1902–1967) was born in Missouri and raised by his grandmother until he was sixteen when he moved to Illinois with his mother and her husband and began to write. Hughes eventually moved to New York City, attended Columbia University, and worked various jobs, including one on a freight ship that sailed down the coast of Africa. In 1921 he saw his first published piece, "The Negro Speaks of Rivers," in the pages of *The Crisis*. Hughes would go on to write eleven plays and numerous works of prose and poetry.

LYNDON BAINES JOHNSON

The 36th president of the United States, Lyndon Baines Johnson (1908–1973) took the office after President Kennedy was assassinated. Born in Stonewall, Texas, Johnson worked as a schoolteacher before joining the House of Representatives in 1937. He is best known for championing the expansion of Civil Rights and a "War on Poverty." He helped pass the Voting Rights Act and also escalated U.S. involvement in the Vietnam War. He did not seek re-election, left office in 1969, and died of a heart attack four years later at his ranch in Texas.

JACK KEROUAC

Jack Kerouac attended Columbia University in New York at the same time as friend and poet Allen Ginsberg (*Howl*). Although Kerouac dropped out, he continued to live in Morningside Heights and became friends with author William S. Burroughs, collaborating with him on the novel *And the Hippos Were Boiled in Their Tanks*. Kerouac's best known work is *On the Road*, which *The New York Times* called "the clearest and most important utterance yet made by the generation Kerouac himself named years ago as 'beat.'"

MARTIN LUTHER KING, JR.

Martin Luther King, Jr. (1929–1968) entered college at the age of fifteen and received a bachelor of arts from Morehouse College. After earning a bachelor of divinity degree and earning his doctorate, he moved to Montgomery, Alabama, in 1954 to become pastor of the Dexter Avenue Baptist Church. Known for his oratorical skills, he led numerous nonviolent protests, including the 1955 bus boycott, the 1963 Birmingham protests, and the March on Washington, where he gave his "I Have a Dream" speech. King was assassinated in Memphis, Tennessee, on April 4, 1968.

GEORGE MARSHALL

General George C. Marshall's (1880–1959) eponymous plan to rebuild Europe in the aftermath of World War II promised funding, which exceeded $12 billion ($125+ billion in 2018), and earned him the 1953 Nobel Peace Prize. Marshall proposed the plan in a speech given at Harvard University in 1947. The plan aimed to thwart the Soviet Union's influence over Western Europe and to accelerate economic development and productivity back to pre-war levels; however, the extent to which the plan deserves credit for affecting growth is disputed among economists.

ARTHUR MILLER

Arthur Miller (1915–2005) was born into a wealthy Manhattan family that had a vacation home in Far Rockaway and a successful business, but his family lost everything when the Stock Market crashed in 1929. They moved to Brooklyn, and Miller delivered bread before school to help his family make ends meet. He eventually attended the University of Michigan, returned to New York City, and wrote his first play, which received poor reviews and closed after a few performances. Undeterred, Miller wrote his next play, *All My Sons*, which won him the Tony Award for Best Author.

AIMEE NEZHUKUMATATHIL

Born in Chicago, Illinois, Aimee Nezhukumatathil (b. 1974) attended The Ohio State University where she received a bachelor's degree in English and a master of fine arts in poetry and creative nonfiction. She received the Diane Middlebrook Poetry Fellowship at the Wisconsin Institute for Creative Writing at University of Wisconsin–Madison and served as the writer-in-residence at the University of Mississippi MFA program from 2016–2017. She is the poetry editor of *Orion* magazine, and her poems have appeared in *Ploughshares*, *Tin House*, and the Best American Poetry series.

FLANNERY O'CONNOR

Flannery O'Connor (1925–1964) was born in Savannah, Georgia. She graduated from the Georgia State College for Women in three years, and in 1946 she was accepted into the Iowa Writers' Workshop. Known for her short stories, she published *A Good Man Is Hard to Find* in 1955 and *Everything That Rises Must Converge* in 1965. O'Connor often wrote in the Southern Gothic style and stated, "Anything that comes out of the South is going to be called grotesque by the Northern reader, unless it is grotesque, in which case it is going to be called realistic."

The Postwar and Civil Rights Eras

I HAVE A DREAM

MARTIN LUTHER KING, JR.

THE MARCH ON WASHINGTON

FOR JOBS AND FREEDOM

AUGUST 28, 1963

Introduction

This overview explains how Americans grappled with both empowerment and disillusionment in the wake of war, and how a national movement for civil rights grew from this angst. After defending their country on the front lines of World War II, African Americans continued to live in a racially divisive society. The text also describes how the political climate impacted literature and journalism, along with other artistic avenues, and how segregation and inequality shifted in the midst of change and progress.

"Communities came together in acts of self-determination to seek equity."

A Global Catastrophe

1   In the 1930s, Italy's Fascists, Germany's Nazis, and Japan's military leadership all aggressively expanded their empires. Expansion by these countries, known as the Axis powers, contributed to the beginning of World War II in 1939. Early in the war, the German forces overwhelmed their enemies, quickly occupying much of Western Europe until only Britain remained unconquered. However, as Axis expansion took place in Europe and Asia, many Americans still believed in the idea of isolationism, especially so soon after World War I.

2   This attitude changed abruptly after the Japanese attack on Pearl Harbor, and the United States mobilized for war against the Axis powers. On the battlefront, U.S. forces turned the tide on the Western Front of Europe and the Pacific, and played a crucial role in the victory of the Allies. At home, United States workers quickly transformed the U.S. economy into the most productive and efficient war machine in the world.

3   *"We are now in this war. We are all in it—all the way. Every single man, woman, and child is a partner in the most tremendous undertaking of our American history."*

4   *—Franklin D. Roosevelt, wartime radio broadcast December 9, 1941*

5   The United States engaged in nearly four years of global warfare, ending with the defeat of the Axis Powers in 1945. The end of the war, which ultimately became the deadliest conflict of all time, left Europe and Japan in tatters. The United States however, experienced an economic boom, cementing its ascent as a global superpower.

The Good War?

6   World War II has become enshrined in the American public memory as "the good war"—a heroic crusade against an evil enemy. But the United States' fight against **Fascism** highlighted the tension between a commitment to democracy and the experience of people of color in America. The Double V Campaign emerged as African American soldiers, fighting in segregated

units, believed that if Americans could defeat Fascism abroad, then they could surely **eradicate** racism and Jim Crow rule at home.

Japanese Americans are moved from their homes into internment camps, supervised by American troops.

7   After Pearl Harbor, the United States forcefully relocated 120,000 people of Japanese ancestry—77,000 of whom were U.S. citizens—into internment camps in early 1942. The renewed migration of African Americans from the South to the big cities in the North and West, continuing the Great Migration, sometimes resulted in racial violence. In Detroit, twenty-five African Americans and nine whites were killed during riots in June 1943. During that same month, riots in Los Angeles occurred after hundreds of U.S. soldiers and sailors attacked a group of young Mexican American men.

Postwar Affluence

8   Wartime production helped restore prosperity to the United States after the long Depression, and postwar legislation continued to fuel the economy. Passed in 1944, the Servicemen's Readjustment Act, more commonly known as the G.I. Bill, expanded opportunities for many Americans. The G.I. Bill provided veterans money for college tuition and weekly unemployment benefits for those seeking a job. Furthermore, the federal government guaranteed loans for veterans who wished to purchase a home, business, or farm. This public policy enabled some veterans unprecedented access to upward mobility, and suddenly, the American Dream was increasingly attainable for a new middle class of white Americans.

Franklin D. Roosevelt signing the G.I. Bill

9   While the G.I. Bill itself did not include racially **discriminatory** language, the execution of the bill was largely unequal. State and local communities chose how to distribute many of the bill's benefits, which resulted in severe inequities in many communities. For example, by the summer of 1947, over 3,000 home loans had been disbursed to veterans. Only two of those loans went to African American veterans. Similarly, veterans of color were denied admission to many "white-only" colleges and institutions, or were simply denied access to G.I. benefits by their local Veterans' Affairs boards. Ultimately, many African American veterans were denied the same economic opportunities that provided **affluence** to their white counterparts.

A Fight for Equity

10   The National Association for the Advancement of Colored People (NAACP) and the Urban League fought against discrimination during the war. Organizer A. Philip Randolph began organizing a march on Washington in 1941 to protest the lack of jobs for African Americans during the war. Randolph met with President Roosevelt, who signed Executive Order 8802, banning discrimination in the defense industry. As a result, Randolph called off the march. Although the military desegregated in 1948, this postwar optimism quickly faded as many veterans were denied benefits from the G.I. Bill, and lawmakers praised the Ku Klux Klan on the floor of Congress. These conditions galvanized the African American community to organize and continue fighting for racial equality.

11   In 1954, the U.S. Supreme Court ruled in its landmark *Brown v. Board of Education* decision that segregated education for whites and blacks was unconstitutional. Progress in desegregating schools was very slow and most schools remained segregated until African American communities took direct action. Inspired by the recent Supreme Court ruling, the NAACP began challenging the segregation of public facilities. On December 1, 1955, the

secretary of the Montgomery, Alabama, NAACP refused to give up her seat on a bus to a white passenger. Rosa Parks's action started a successful, year-long boycott of the city's segregated buses. Leaders such as Parks, a young minister named Martin Luther King Jr., and Ralph Abernathy organized the African American community and advocated for nonviolent direct action through their powerful actions, speeches, and writing.

12   Following the success of the Montgomery Bus Boycott, King and other civil rights leaders soon engaged in a strategic campaign of nonviolent resistance and civil disobedience to end segregation and secure voting rights. In 1957, nine black students attempted to integrate Central High School in Little Rock, Arkansas. When state authorities and a mob blocked the entrance, President Eisenhower called in federal troops to ensure that students could attend school according to the law. College students in Greensboro, North Carolina, engaged in another version of nonviolent resistance when they staged a "sit-in" at a segregated lunch counter. The four young men refused to move from their stool at the counter without being served. Leaders also used tactics such as peaceful marches. In 1963, A. Philip Randolph began to work towards another march, alongside his chief aid Bayard Rustin. This time, he did not call off his efforts, and there was a massive public demonstration, the "March on Washington for Freedom and Jobs." There, Martin Luther King Jr. delivered his famous "I Have a Dream" speech to a crowd of over 250,000 people.

13   African American communities continued to fight for equal treatment under the law, eventually leading to landmark legislation, such as the Civil Rights Act of 1964 and the Voting Rights Act of 1965. While the new legislation offered protections against discrimination in employment and nullified restrictive Jim Crow voting laws, African American communities continued their efforts to make sure that federal legislation was followed. Many of these efforts continue to the present day.

A. Philip Randolph (left) and Bayard Rustin (right) appearing before a Senate subcommittee in 1966

14 **Major Concepts**

- **The United States and the World**—In 1941, aggression by the Axis Powers led the United States to enter World War II. During this period, American writers examined both wartime struggles and postwar anxieties.

- **Postwar Optimism and Pessimism**—The war united many Americans in the belief that they were saving the world against the evil forces of Fascism in Germany, Italy, and Japan. The G.I. Bill allowed millions of Americans to enter the middle class. Yet the carnage and horror of wartime atrocities, such as the firebombing of Dresden, the Nazi Death Camps, and the use of the atomic bomb on Hiroshima and Nagasaki, left many Americans searching for meaning. The denial of equal opportunities to minority groups, such as African Americans, Latinos, Japanese Americans, and Native Americans, led to further alienation.

- **Suburbia**—Despite the importance of cities in the development of the United States, a deep distrust of urban life has also been a part of the U.S. character. By 1900, U.S. cities were ringed with suburbs. The growth of suburbia continued to accelerate throughout the twentieth century. For millions of people in the United States, a home in the suburbs came to symbolize the American dream. Nevertheless, some writers have depicted suburbia as a cultural wasteland inhabited by conformists. John Cheever and John Updike are two writers who have explored the culture of suburbs in the United States.

- **Civil Rights Era**—African American veterans returned home to segregation and inequality after fighting for democracy and freedom abroad. Communities came together in acts of self-determination to seek equity. Writers and journalists during this period advocated for change in order to move the country to support an end to segregation.

Style & Form

15 **New Journalism**

- Journalists began to experiment with the form and function of reporting in order to more fully capture the nuance of current events. Writers such as John Hersey, Joan Didion, and Tom Wolfe began to incorporate devices from literature into their feature articles for newspapers and magazines.

- New journalists borrowed literary techniques such as telling a story in scenes, incorporating dialogue, developing the voice of the narrator, presenting the story through various points of view, and employing **characterization** techniques to bring the subject alive to the reader.

16 **Postwar Realism**

- Postwar legislation dramatically changed American society and American literature with it. Playwrights such as Lorraine Hansberry and Arthur Miller sought to capture the experience of the new middle class, and included new voices and themes to reflect the various experiences within an upwardly mobile society.

17 **Beat Fiction and Poetry**

- Beat writers often found it difficult to connect with the optimism of the 1950s and rejected suburban complacency. Known as the Beat Generation, writers such as Allen Ginsberg and Jack Kerouac engaged in experimental forms of writing, attempting to capture the reality of each moment on the page, often with very little planning or revision.

18 **Aspirational Rhetoric**

- As victors of World War II, Americans developed a new consciousness as protectors of freedom and democracy. This attitude found its way into the writings of politicians, journalists, and activists. Writing from this time appealed to a higher moral purpose and often charged the United States with a duty to spread freedom, democracy, and free trade at home and abroad.

- Biblical rhetoric was often employed by leaders within the civil rights movement. For example, Martin Luther King Jr. frequently wove imagery and context from the Bible into his speeches.

19 The period after World War II and into the civil rights movement was full of changes for the United States and the world, and the social and political actions of this time remain relevant. Communities continue to grapple with the implications of landmark legislation and decisions, such as the Civil Rights Acts of 1964, and modern politicians evoke the rhetoric of the civil rights movement. How do you feel the postwar and civil rights eras continue to shape society today?

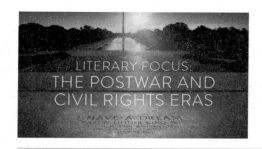

Literary Focus: The Postwar and Civil Rights Eras

Read "Literary Focus: The Postwar and Civil Rights Eras." After you read, complete the Think Questions below.

THINK QUESTIONS

1. Why did Americans change their minds about isolationism following the Japanese attack on Pearl Harbor? Explain, citing evidence from the text.

2. What is the disparity between WWII's nickname, "the good war," and the reality for marginalized citizens in American society? Explain, citing evidence from the text.

3. In which ways did the desegregation of the U.S. military in 1948 symbolize that it was just the beginning of the civil rights movement? Support your response with evidence from the text.

4. Use context clues to determine the meaning of **affluence** as it is used in the text. Write your best definition of *affluence* here, using evidence to explain your understanding.

5. What is the meaning of the word **discriminatory** as it is used in the text? Write your best definition of *discriminatory* here, along with a brief explanation of how you arrived at its meaning. Then, check a dictionary to confirm your understanding.

Please note that excerpts and passages in the StudySync® library and this workbook are intended as touchstones to generate interest in an author's work. The excerpts and passages do not substitute for the reading of entire texts, and StudySync® strongly recommends that students seek out and purchase the whole literary or informational work in order to experience it as the author intended. Links to online resellers are available in our digital library. In addition, complete works may be ordered through an authorized reseller by filling out and returning to StudySync® the order form enclosed in this workbook.

Reading & Writing Companion

7

Hiroshima

INFORMATIONAL TEXT
John Hersey
1946

Introduction

John Hersey (1914–1993) collected eyewitness accounts of life in Hiroshima after the detonation of a nuclear bomb and intended to release them in serial form in *The New Yorker* until the editors made a last-minute decision to devote an entire issue to Hersey's reporting. The 1946 article was an immediate sensation, giving Americans their first real understanding of the impact of a nuclear weapon. In this excerpt, Hersey describes some of the aftermath of the bombing.

"The bomb had not only left the underground organs of plants intact; it had stimulated them."

Copyright © BookheadEd Learning, LLC

Excerpt from *Chapter Four: Panic Grass and Feverfew*

NOTES

1   The hospitals and aid stations around Hiroshima were so crowded in the first weeks after the bombing and staffs were so variable, depending on their health and on the unpredictable arrival of outside help, that patients had to be constantly shifted from place to place. Miss Sasaki, who had already been moved three times, twice by ship, was taken at the end of August to an engineering school, also at Hatsukaichi[1]. Because her leg did not improve but swelled more and more, the doctors at the school bound it with **crude** splints and took her by car, on September 9th, to the Red Cross Hospital in Hiroshima. This was the first chance she had had to look at the ruins of Hiroshima; the last time she had been carried through the city's streets, she had been hovering on the edge of unconsciousness. Even though the wreckage had been described to her, and though she was still in pain, the sight horrified and amazed her, and there was something she noticed about it that particularly gave her the creeps. Over everything—up through the wreckage of the city, in gutters, along the riverbanks, tangled among tiles and tin roofing, climbing on charred tree trunks—was a blanket of fresh, vivid, lush, optimistic green; the verdancy rose even from the foundations of ruined houses. Weeds already hid the ashes, and wild flowers were in bloom among the city's bones. The bomb had not only left the underground organs of plants intact; it had **stimulated** them. Everywhere were bluets and Spanish bayonets, goosefoot, morning glories and day lilies, the hairy-fruited bean, purslane and clotbur and sesame and panic grass and feverfew. Especially in a circle at the center, sickle senna grew in extraordinary **regeneration**, not only standing among the charred remnants of the same plant but pushing up in new places, among bricks and through cracks in the asphalt. It actually seemed as if a load of sickle-senna seed had been dropped along with the bomb. . . .

2   A year after the bomb was dropped, Miss Sasaki was a cripple; Mrs. Nakamura was **destitute**; Father Kleinsorge was back in the hospital; Dr. Sasaki was not capable of the work he once could do; Dr. Fujii had lost the thirty-room hospital it

---

1. **Hatsukaichi** a city near Hiroshima

took him many years to acquire, and had no prospects of rebuilding it; Mr. Tanimoto's church had been ruined and he no longer had his exceptional vitality. The lives of these six people, among the luckiest in Hiroshima, would never be the same. What they thought of their experiences and of the use of the atomic bomb was, of course, not unanimous. One feeling they did seem to share, however, was a **curious** kind of elated community spirit, something like that of the Londoners after their blitz—a pride in the way they and their fellow survivors had stood up to a dreadful ordeal. Just before the anniversary, Mr. Tanimoto wrote in a letter to an American some words which expressed this feeling: "What a heartbreaking scene this was the first night! About midnight I landed on the riverbank. So many injured people lied on the ground that I made my way by striding over them. Repeating 'Excuse me,' I forwarded and carried a tub of water with me and gave a cup of water to each of them. They raised their upper bodies slowly and accepted a cup of water with a bow and drunk quietly and, spilling any remnants gave back a cup with hearty expression of their thankfulness, and said, 'I couldn't help my sister, who was buried under the house, because I had to take care of my mother who got a deep wound on her eye and our house soon set fire and we hardly escaped. Look, I lost my home, my family, and at last myself bitterly injured. But now I have gotten my mind to dedicate what I have and to complete the war for our country's sake.' Thus they pledged to me, even women and children did the same. Being entirely tired I lied down on the ground among them, but couldn't sleep at all. Next morning I found many men and women dead, whom I gave water last night. But to my great surprise, I never heard any one cried in disorder, even though they suffered in great agony. They died in silence, with no grudge, setting their teeth to bear it. All for the country." . . .

3   It would be impossible to say what horrors were embedded in the minds of the children who lived through the day of the bombing in Hiroshima. On the surface their recollections, months after the disasters, were of an exhilarating adventure. Toshio Nakamura, who was ten at the time of the bombing, was soon able to talk freely, even gaily, about the experience, and a few weeks before the anniversary he wrote the following matter-of-fact essay for his teacher at No-bori-cho Primary School: "The day before the bomb, I went for a swim. In the morning, I was eating peanuts. I saw a light. I was knocked to little sister's sleeping place. When we were saved, I could only see as far as the tram. My mother and I started to pack our things. The neighbors were walking around burned and bleeding. Hataya-*san* told me to run away with her. I said I wanted to wait for my mother. We went to the park. A whirlwind came. At night a gas tank burned and I saw the reflection in the river. We stayed in the park one night. Next day I went to Taiko Bridge and met my girl friends Kikuki and Murakami. They were looking for their mothers. But Kikuki's mother was wounded and Murakami's mother, alas, was dead."

Excerpted from *Hiroshima* by John Hersey, published by Ishi Press.

Copyright © BookheadEd Learning, LLC

WRITE

EXPLANATORY: In *Hiroshima*, Hersey pioneered the use of literary techniques in a nonfiction piece. Identify and analyze Hersey's use of these techniques to convey the experiences of the survivors of the Hiroshima bombing. How does the author use literary techniques to address this tragedy? Cite evidence from the text to justify and explain your analysis.

Please note that excerpts and passages in the StudySync® library and this workbook are intended as touchstones to generate interest in an author's work. The excerpts and passages do not substitute for the reading of entire texts, and StudySync® strongly recommends that students seek out and purchase the whole literary or informational work in order to experience it as the author intended. Links to online resellers are available in our digital library. In addition, complete works may be ordered through an authorized reseller by filling out and returning to StudySync® the order form enclosed in this workbook.

Reading & Writing Companion

11

A Good Man Is Hard to Find

FICTION
Flannery O'Connor
1953

Introduction

Flannery O'Connor (1925–1964) was one of a kind. A lifelong resident of Milledgeville, Georgia, and a devout Catholic, she produced in her short career some of the best American writing of the postwar period. Her style of Southern Gothic writing was characterized by elements of religion, morality, violence, and redemption. In this, her most famous story, a disgruntled family on a grudging trip to Florida takes a detour with devastating consequences. Have they met the Devil himself? Or merely wandered into a predestined fate?

"... Why you're one of my babies. You're one of my own children!"

> Note: The text you are about to read contains offensive language. Remember to be mindful of the thoughts and feelings of your peers as you read and discuss this text. Please consult your teacher for additional guidance and support.

NOTES

1　THE GRANDMOTHER didn't want to go to Florida. She wanted to visit some of her connections in east Tennessee and she was seizing at every chance to change Bailey's mind. Bailey was the son she lived with, her only boy. He was sitting on the edge of his chair at the table, bent over the orange sports section of the Journal. "Now look here, Bailey," she said, "see here, read this," and she stood with one hand on her thin hip and the other rattling the newspaper at his bald head. "Here this fellow that calls himself The Misfit is aloose from the Federal Pen and headed toward Florida and you read here what it says he did to these people. Just you read it. I wouldn't take my children in any direction with a criminal like that aloose in it. I couldn't answer to my conscience if I did."

2　Bailey didn't look up from his reading so she wheeled around then and faced the children's mother, a young woman in slacks, whose face was as broad and innocent as a cabbage and was tied around with a green head-kerchief that had two points on the top like rabbit's ears. She was sitting on the sofa, feeding the baby his apricots out of a jar. "The children have been to Florida before," the old lady said. "You all ought to take them somewhere else for a change so they would see different parts of the world and be broad. They never have been to east Tennessee."

3　The children's mother didn't seem to hear her but the eight-year-old boy, John Wesley, a stocky child with glasses, said, "If you don't want to go to Florida, why dontcha stay at home?" He and the little girl, June Star, were reading the funny papers on the floor.

4　"She wouldn't stay at home to be queen for a day," June Star said without raising her yellow head.

5　"Yes and what would you do if this fellow, The Misfit, caught you?" the grandmother asked.

Skill:
Story Structure

The grandmother is determined to get what she wants. She points out that a criminal has escaped in Florida to manipulate her son. She even brings up her conscience. This creates tension and foreshadows the ending of the story.

NOTES

6 "I'd smack his face," John Wesley said.

7 "She wouldn't stay at home for a million bucks," June Star said. "Afraid she'd miss something. She has to go everywhere we go."

8 "All right, Miss," the grandmother said. "Just remember that the next time you want me to curl your hair."

9 June Star said her hair was naturally curly.

10 The next morning the grandmother was the first one in the car, ready to go. She had her big black valise that looked like the head of a hippopotamus in one corner, and underneath it she was hiding a basket with Pitty Sing, the cat, in it. She didn't intend for the cat to be left alone in the house for three days because he would miss her too much and she was afraid he might brush against one of the gas burners and accidentally asphyxiate himself. Her son, Bailey, didn't like to arrive at a motel with a cat.

11 She sat in the middle of the back seat with John Wesley and June Star on either side of her. Bailey and the children's mother and the baby sat in front and they left Atlanta at eight forty-five with the mileage on the car at 55890. The grandmother wrote this down because she thought it would be interesting to say how many miles they had been when they got back. It took them twenty minutes to reach the outskirts of the city.

12 The old lady settled herself comfortably, removing her white cotton gloves and putting them up with her purse on the shelf in front of the back window. The children's mother still had on slacks and still had her head tied up in a green kerchief, but the grandmother had on a navy blue straw sailor hat with a bunch of white violets on the brim and a navy blue dress with a small white dot in the print. Her collars and cuffs were white organdy trimmed with lace and at her neckline she had pinned a purple spray of cloth violets containing a sachet. In case of an accident, anyone seeing her dead on the highway would know at once that she was a lady.

13 She said she thought it was going to be a good day for driving, neither too hot nor too cold, and she cautioned Bailey that the speed limit was fifty-five miles an hour and that the patrolmen hid themselves behind billboards and small clumps of trees and sped out after you before you had a chance to slow down. She pointed out interesting details of the scenery: Stone Mountain; the blue granite that in some places came up to both sides of the highway; the brilliant red clay banks slightly streaked with purple; and the various crops that made rows of green lace-work on the ground. The trees were full of silver-white sunlight and the meanest of them sparkled. The children were reading comic magazines and their mother had gone back to sleep.

14 "Let's go through Georgia fast so we won't have to look at it much," John Wesley said.

15   "If I were a little boy," said the grandmother, "I wouldn't talk about my native state that way. Tennessee has the mountains and Georgia has the hills."

16   "Tennessee is just a hillbilly dumping ground," John Wesley said, "and Georgia is a lousy state too."

17   "You said it," June Star said.

18   "In my time," said the grandmother, folding her thin veined fingers, "children were more respectful of their native states and their parents and everything else. People did right then. Oh look at the cute little pickaninny!"[1] she said and pointed to a Negro child standing in the door of a shack. "Wouldn't that make a picture, now?" she asked and they all turned and looked at the little Negro out of the back window. He waved.

19   "He didn't have any britches on," June Star said.

20   "He probably didn't have any," the grandmother explained. "Little n-----s in the country don't have things like we do. If I could paint, I'd paint that picture," she said.

21   The children exchanged comic books.

22   The grandmother offered to hold the baby and the children's mother passed him over the front seat to her. She set him on her knee and bounced him and told him about the things they were passing. She rolled her eyes and screwed up her mouth and stuck her leathery thin face into his smooth bland one. Occasionally he gave her a faraway smile. They passed a large cotton field with five or six graves fenced in the middle of it, like a small island. "Look at the graveyard!" the grandmother said, pointing it out. "That was the old family burying ground. That belonged to the plantation."

23   "Where's the plantation?" John Wesley asked.

24   "Gone With the Wind," said the grandmother. "Ha. Ha."

25   When the children finished all the comic books they had brought, they opened the lunch and ate it. The grandmother ate a peanut butter sandwich and an olive and would not let the children throw the box and the paper napkins out the window. When there was nothing else to do they played a game by choosing a cloud and making the other two guess what shape it suggested. John Wesley took one the shape of a cow and June Star guessed a cow and John Wesley said, no, an automobile, and June Star said he didn't play fair, and they began to slap each other over the grandmother.

---

1. **pickaninny** an old-fashioned term for an African American child, now considered a racist slur

26 The grandmother said she would tell them a story if they would keep quiet. When she told a story, she rolled her eyes and waved her head and was very dramatic. She said once when she was a maiden lady she had been courted by a Mr. Edgar Atkins Teagarden from Jasper, Georgia. She said he was a very good-looking man and a gentleman and that he brought her a watermelon every Saturday afternoon with his initials cut in it, E. A. T. Well, one Saturday, she said, Mr. Teagarden brought the watermelon and there was nobody at home and he left it on the front porch and returned in his buggy to Jasper, but she never got the watermelon, she said, because a n----- boy ate it when he saw the initials, E. A. T.! This story tickled John Wesley's funny bone and he giggled and giggled but June Star didn't think it was any good. She said she wouldn't marry a man that just brought her a watermelon on Saturday. The grandmother said she would have done well to marry Mr. Teagarden because he was a gentleman and had bought Coca-Cola stock when it first came out and that he had died only a few years ago, a very wealthy man.

27 They stopped at The Tower for barbecued sandwiches. The Tower was a part stucco and part wood filling station and dance hall set in a clearing outside of Timothy. A fat man named Red Sammy Butts ran it and there were signs stuck here and there on the building and for miles up and down the highway saying, TRY RED SAMMY'S FAMOUS BARBECUE. NONE LIKE FAMOUS RED SAMMY'S! RED SAM! THE FAT BOY WITH THE HAPPY LAUGH. A VETERAN! RED SAMMY'S YOUR MAN!

28 Red Sammy was lying on the bare ground outside The Tower with his head under a truck while a gray monkey about a foot high, chained to a small chinaberry tree, chattered nearby. The monkey sprang back into the tree and got on the highest limb as soon as he saw the children jump out of the car and run toward him.

29 Inside, The Tower was a long dark room with a counter at one end and tables at the other and dancing space in the middle. They all sat down at a board table next to the nickelodeon and Red Sam's wife, a tall burnt-brown woman with hair and eyes lighter than her skin, came and took their order. The children's mother put a dime in the machine and played "The Tennessee Waltz," and the grandmother said that tune always made her want to dance. She asked Bailey if he would like to dance but he only glared at her. He didn't have a naturally sunny **disposition** like she did and trips made him nervous. The grandmother's brown eyes were very bright. She swayed her head from side to side and pretended she was dancing in her chair. June Star said play something she could tap to so the children's mother put in another dime and played a fast number and June Star stepped out onto the dance floor and did her tap routine.

30 "Ain't she cute?" Red Sam's wife said, leaning over the counter. "Would you like to come be my little girl?"

Skill: Connotation and Denotation

The word glared has a negative connotation and is in contrast with the words sunny and bright. I think Bailey is annoyed by the grandmother, and she seems to be pretending everything is cheerful.

31   "No I certainly wouldn't," June Star said. "I wouldn't live in a broken-down place like this for a minion bucks!" and she ran back to the table.

32   "Ain't she cute?" the woman repeated, stretching her mouth politely.

33   "Arn't you ashamed?" hissed the grandmother.

34   Red Sam came in and told his wife to quit lounging on the counter and hurry up with these people's order. His khaki trousers reached just to his hip bones and his stomach hung over them like a sack of meal swaying under his shirt. He came over and sat down at a table nearby and let out a combination sigh and yodel. "You can't win," he said. "You can't win," and he wiped his sweating red face off with a gray handkerchief. "These days you don't know who to trust," he said. "Ain't that the truth?"

35   "People are certainly not nice like they used to be," said the grandmother.

36   "Two fellers come in here last week," Red Sammy said, "driving a Chrysler. It was a old beat-up car but it was a good one and these boys looked all right to me. Said they worked at the mill and you know I let them fellers charge the gas they bought? Now why did I do that?"

37   "Because you're a good man!" the grandmother said at once.

38   "Yes'm, I suppose so," Red Sam said as if he were struck with this answer.

39   His wife brought the orders, carrying the five plates all at once without a tray, two in each hand and one balanced on her arm. "It isn't a soul in this green world of God's that you can trust," she said. "And I don't count nobody out of that, not nobody," she repeated, looking at Red Sammy.

40   "Did you read about that criminal, The Misfit, that's escaped?" asked the grandmother.

41   "I wouldn't be a bit surprised if he didn't attack this place right here," said the woman. "If he hears about it being here, I wouldn't be none surprised to see him. If he hears it's two cent in the cash register, I wouldn't be a tall surprised if he . . ."

42   "That'll do," Red Sam said. "Go bring these people their Co'-Colas," and the woman went off to get the rest of the order.

43   "A good man is hard to find," Red Sammy said. "Everything is getting terrible. I remember the day you could go off and leave your screen door unlatched. Not no more."

44   He and the grandmother discussed better times. The old lady said that in her opinion Europe was entirely to blame for the way things were now. She said the way Europe acted you would think we were made of money and Red

Skill:
Story Structure

The Misfit is mentioned again, and the wife says that he would "attack" them. Red Sam feels that there are few good men and that the world is terrible. This is a dark view of humanity, which is sad and scary.

Please note that excerpts and passages in the StudySync® library and this workbook are intended as touchstones to generate interest in an author's work. The excerpts and passages do not substitute for the reading of entire texts, and StudySync® strongly recommends that students seek out and purchase the whole literary or informational work in order to experience it as the author intended. Links to online resellers are available in our digital library. In addition, complete works may be ordered through an authorized reseller by filling out and returning to StudySync® the order form enclosed in this workbook.

Reading & Writing Companion   17

Sam said it was no use talking about it, she was exactly right. The children ran outside into the white sunlight and looked at the monkey in the lacy chinaberry tree. He was busy catching fleas on himself and biting each one carefully between his teeth as if it were a **delicacy**.

45 They drove off again into the hot afternoon. The grandmother took cat naps and woke up every few minutes with her own snoring. Outside of Toombsboro she woke up and recalled an old plantation that she had visited in this neighborhood once when she was a young lady. She said the house had six white columns across the front and that there was an avenue of oaks leading up to it and two little wooden trellis arbors on either side in front where you sat down with your suitor after a stroll in the garden. She recalled exactly which road to turn off to get to it. She knew that Bailey would not be willing to lose any time looking at an old house, but the more she talked about it, the more she wanted to see it once again and find out if the little twin arbors were still standing. "There was a secret panel in this house," she said craftily, not telling the truth but wishing that she were, "and the story went that all the family silver was hidden in it when Sherman came through but it was never found . . ."

46 "Hey!" John Wesley said. "Let's go see it! We'll find it! We'll poke all the woodwork and find it! Who lives there? Where do you turn off at? Hey Pop, can't we turn off there?"

47 "We never have seen a house with a secret panel!" June Star shrieked. "Let's go to the house with the secret panel! Hey Pop, can't we go see the house with the secret panel!"

48 "It's not far from here, I know," the grandmother said. "It wouldn't take over twenty minutes."

49 Bailey was looking straight ahead. His jaw was as rigid as a horseshoe. "No," he said.

50 The children began to yell and scream that they wanted to see the house with the secret panel. John Wesley kicked the back of the front seat and June Star hung over her mother's shoulder and whined desperately into her ear that they never had any fun even on their vacation, that they could never do what THEY wanted to do. The baby began to scream and John Wesley kicked the back of the seat so hard that his father could feel the blows in his kidney.

51 "All right!" he shouted and drew the car to a stop at the side of the road. "Will you all shut up? Will you all just shut up for one second? If you don't shut up, we won't go anywhere."

52 "It would be very educational for them," the grandmother murmured.

53 "All right," Bailey said, "but get this: this is the only time we're going to stop for anything like this. This is the one and only time."

54 "The dirt road that you have to turn down is about a mile back," the grandmother directed. "I marked it when we passed."

55 "A dirt road," Bailey groaned.

56 After they had turned around and were headed toward the dirt road, the grandmother recalled other points about the house, the beautiful glass over the front doorway and the candle-lamp in the hall. John Wesley said that the secret panel was probably in the fireplace.

57 "You can't go inside this house," Bailey said. "You don't know who lives there."

58 "While you all talk to the people in front, I'll run around behind and get in a window," John Wesley suggested.

59 "We'll all stay in the car," his mother said. They turned onto the dirt road and the car raced roughly along in a swirl of pink dust. The grandmother recalled the times when there were no paved roads and thirty miles was a day's journey. The dirt road was hilly and there were sudden washes in it and sharp curves on dangerous embankments. All at once they would be on a hill, looking down over the blue tops of trees for miles around, then the next minute, they would be in a red depression with the dust-coated trees looking down on them.

60 "This place had better turn up in a minute," Bailey said, "or I'm going to turn around."

61 The road looked as if no one had traveled on it in months.

62 "It's not much farther," the grandmother said and just as she said it, a horrible thought came to her. The thought was so embarrassing that she turned red in the face and her eyes dilated and her feet jumped up, upsetting her valise in the corner. The instant the valise moved, the newspaper top she had over the basket under it rose with a snarl and Pitty Sing, the cat, sprang onto Bailey's shoulder.

63 The children were thrown to the floor and their mother, clutching the baby, was thrown out the door onto the ground; the old lady was thrown into the front seat. The car turned over once and landed right-side-up in a gulch off the side of the road. Bailey remained in the driver's seat with the cat—gray-striped with a broad white face and an orange nose—clinging to his neck like a caterpillar.

64 As soon as the children saw they could move their arms and legs, they scrambled out of the car, shouting, "We've had an ACCIDENT!" The

grandmother was curled up under the dashboard, hoping she was injured so that Bailey's wrath would not come down on her all at once. The horrible thought she had had before the accident was that the house she had remembered so vividly was not in Georgia but in Tennessee.

65 Bailey removed the cat from his neck with both hands and flung it out the window against the side of a pine tree. Then he got out of the car and started looking for the children's mother. She was sitting against the side of the red gutted ditch, holding the screaming baby, but she only had a cut down her face and a broken shoulder. "We've had an ACCIDENT!" the children screamed in a frenzy of delight.

66 "But nobody's killed," June Star said with disappointment as the grandmother limped out of the car, her hat still pinned to her head but the broken front brim standing up at a **jaunty** angle and the violet spray hanging off the side. They all sat down in the ditch, except the children, to recover from the shock. They were all shaking.

67 "Maybe a car will come along," said the children's mother hoarsely.

68 "I believe I have injured an organ," said the grandmother, pressing her side, but no one answered her. Bailey's teeth were clattering. He had on a yellow sport shirt with bright blue parrots designed in it and his face was as yellow as the shirt. The grandmother decided that she would not mention that the house was in Tennessee.

69 The road was about ten feet above and they could see only the tops of the trees on the other side of it. Behind the ditch they were sitting in there were more woods, tall and dark and deep. In a few minutes they saw a car some distance away on top of a hill, coming slowly as if the occupants were watching them. The grandmother stood up and waved both arms dramatically to attract their attention. The car continued to come on slowly, disappeared around a bend and appeared again, moving even slower, on top of the hill they had gone over. It was a big black battered hearse-like automobile. There were three men in it.

70 It came to a stop just over them and for some minutes, the driver looked down with a steady expressionless gaze to where they were sitting, and didn't speak. Then he turned his head and muttered something to the other two and they got out. One was a fat boy in black trousers and a red sweat shirt with a silver stallion embossed on the front of it. He moved around on the right side of them and stood staring, his mouth partly open in a kind of loose grin. The other had on khaki pants and a blue striped coat and a gray hat pulled down very low, hiding most of his face. He came around slowly on the left side. Neither spoke.

71 The driver got out of the car and stood by the side of it, looking down at them. He was an older man than the other two. His hair was just beginning to gray and he wore silver-rimmed spectacles that gave him a scholarly look. He had a long creased face and didn't have on any shirt or undershirt. He had on blue jeans that were too tight for him and was holding a black hat and a gun. The two boys also had guns.

72 "We've had an ACCIDENT!" the children screamed.

73 The grandmother had the peculiar feeling that the bespectacled man was someone she knew. His face was as familiar to her as if she had known him all her life but she could not recall who he was. He moved away from the car and began to come down the embankment, placing his feet carefully so that he wouldn't slip. He had on tan and white shoes and no socks, and his ankles were red and thin. "Good afternoon," he said. "I see you all had you a little spill."

74 "We turned over twice!" said the grandmother.

75 "Oncet," he corrected. "We seen it happen. Try their car and see will it run, Hiram," he said quietly to the boy with the gray hat.

76 "What you got that gun for?" John Wesley asked. "Whatcha gonna do with that gun?"

77 "Lady," the man said to the children's mother, "would you mind calling them children to sit down by you? Children make me nervous. I want all you all to sit down right together there where you're at."

78 "What are you telling US what to do for?" June Star asked.

79 Behind them the line of woods gaped like a dark open mouth. "Come here," said their mother.

80 "Look here now," Bailey began suddenly, "we're in a predicament! We're in . . ."

81 The grandmother shrieked. She scrambled to her feet and stood staring. "You're The Misfit!" she said. "I recognized you at once!"

82 "Yes'm," the man said, smiling slightly as if he were pleased in spite of himself to be known, "but it would have been better for all of you, lady, if you hadn't of reckernized me."

83 Bailey turned his head sharply and said something to his mother that shocked even the children. The old lady began to cry and The Misfit reddened.

84 "Lady," he said, "don't you get upset. Sometimes a man says things he don't mean. I don't reckon he meant to talk to you thataway."

Please note that excerpts and passages in the StudySync® library and this workbook are intended as touchstones to generate interest in an author's work. The excerpts and passages do not substitute for the reading of entire texts, and StudySync® strongly recommends that students seek out and purchase the whole literary or informational work in order to experience it as the author intended. Links to online resellers are available in our digital library. In addition, complete works may be ordered through an authorized reseller by filling out and returning to StudySync® the order form enclosed in this workbook.

Reading & Writing Companion   21

85 "You wouldn't shoot a lady, would you?" the grandmother said and removed a clean handkerchief from her cuff and began to slap at her eyes with it.

86 The Misfit pointed the toe of his shoe into the ground and made a little hole and then covered it up again. "I would hate to have to," he said.

87 "Listen," the grandmother almost screamed, "I know you're a good man. You don't look a bit like you have common blood. I know you must come from nice people!"

88 "Yes mam," he said, "finest people in the world." When he smiled he showed a row of strong white teeth. "God never made a finer woman than my mother and my daddy's heart was pure gold," he said. The boy with the red sweat shirt had come around behind them and was standing with his gun at his hip. The Misfit squatted down on the ground. "Watch them children, Bobby Lee," he said. "You know they make me nervous." He looked at the six of them huddled together in front of him and he seemed to be embarrassed as if he couldn't think of anything to say. "Ain't a cloud in the sky," he remarked, looking up at it. "Don't see no sun but don't see no cloud neither."

89 "Yes, it's a beautiful day," said the grandmother. "Listen," she said, "you shouldn't call yourself The Misfit because I know you're a good man at heart. I can just look at you and tell."

90 "Hush!" Bailey yelled. "Hush! Everybody shut up and let me handle this!" He was squatting in the position of a runner about to sprint forward but he didn't move.

91 "I prechate that, lady," The Misfit said and drew a little circle in the ground with the butt of his gun.

92 "It'll take a half a hour to fix this here car," Hiram called, looking over the raised hood of it.

93 "Well, first you and Bobby Lee get him and that little boy to step over yonder with you," The Misfit said, pointing to Bailey and John Wesley. "The boys want to ast you some-thing," he said to Bailey. "Would you mind stepping back in them woods there with them?"

94 "Listen," Bailey began, "we're in a terrible predicament! Nobody realizes what this is," and his voice cracked. His eyes were as blue and intense as the parrots in his shirt and he remained perfectly still.

95 The grandmother reached up to adjust her hat brim as if she were going to the woods with him but it came off in her hand. She stood staring at it and after a second she let it fall on the ground. Hiram pulled Bailey up by the arm as if he were assisting an old man. John Wesley caught hold of his father's

hand and Bobby Lee followed. They went off toward the woods and just as they reached the dark edge, Bailey turned and supporting himself against a gray naked pine trunk, he shouted, "I'll be back in a minute, Mamma, wait on me!"

96   "Come back this instant!" his mother shrilled but they all disappeared into the woods.

97   "Bailey Boy!" the grandmother called in a tragic voice but she found she was looking at The Misfit squatting on the ground in front of her. "I just know you're a good man," she said desperately. "You're not a bit common!"

98   "Nome, I ain't a good man," The Misfit said after a second as if he had considered her statement carefully, "but I ain't the worst in the world neither. My daddy said I was a different breed of dog from my brothers and sisters. 'You know,' Daddy said, 'it's some that can live their whole life out without asking about it and it's others has to know why it is, and this boy is one of the latters. He's going to be into every-thing!'" He put on his black hat and looked up suddenly and then away deep into the woods as if he were embarrassed again. "I'm sorry I don't have on a shirt before you ladies," he said, hunching his shoulders slightly. "We buried our clothes that we had on when we escaped and we're just making do until we can get better. We borrowed these from some folks we met," he explained.

99   "That's perfectly all right," the grandmother said. "Maybe Bailey has an extra shirt in his suitcase."

100   "I'll look and see terrectly," The Misfit said.

101   "Where are they taking him?" the children's mother screamed.

102   "Daddy was a card himself," The Misfit said. "You couldn't put anything over on him. He never got in trouble with the Authorities though. Just had the knack of handling them."

103   "You could be honest too if you'd only try," said the grandmother. "Think how wonderful it would be to settle down and live a comfortable life and not have to think about some-body chasing you all the time."

104   The Misfit kept scratching in the ground with the butt of his gun as if he were thinking about it. "Yes'm, somebody is always after you," he murmured.

105   The grandmother noticed how thin his shoulder blades were just behind his hat because she was standing up looking down on him. "Do you ever pray?" she asked.

106   He shook his head. All she saw was the black hat wiggle between his shoulder blades. "Nome," he said.

107   There was a pistol shot from the woods, followed closely by another. Then silence. The old lady's head jerked around. She could hear the wind move through the tree tops like a long satisfied insuck of breath. "Bailey Boy!" she called.

108   "I was a gospel singer for a while," The Misfit said. "I been most everything. Been in the arm service, both land and sea, at home and abroad, been twict married, been an undertaker, been with the railroads, plowed Mother Earth, been in a tornado, seen a man burnt alive oncet," and he looked up at the children's mother and the little girl who were sitting close together, their faces white and their eyes glassy; "I even seen a woman flogged," he said.

109   "Pray, pray," the grandmother began, "pray, pray . . ."

110   "I never was a bad boy that I remember of," The Misfit said in an almost dreamy voice, "but somewheres along the line I done something wrong and got sent to the **penitentiary.** I was buried alive," and he looked up and held her attention to him by a steady stare.

111   "That's when you should have started to pray," she said. "What did you do to get sent to the penitentiary that first time?"

112   "Turn to the right, it was a wall," The Misfit said, looking up again at the cloudless sky. "Turn to the left, it was a wall. Look up it was a ceiling, look down it was a floor. I forget what I done, lady. I set there and set there, trying to remember what it was I done and I ain't recalled it to this day. Oncet in a while, I would think it was coming to me, but it never come."

113   "Maybe they put you in by mistake," the old lady said vaguely.

114   "Nome," he said. "It wasn't no mistake. They had the papers on me."

115   "You must have stolen something," she said.

116   The Misfit sneered slightly. "Nobody had nothing I wanted," he said. "It was a head-doctor at the penitentiary said what I had done was kill my daddy but I known that for a lie. My daddy died in nineteen ought nineteen of the epidemic flu and I never had a thing to do with it. He was buried in the Mount Hopewell Baptist churchyard and you can go there and see for yourself."

117   "If you would pray," the old lady said, "Jesus would help you."

118   "That's right," The Misfit said.

119   "Well then, why don't you pray?" she asked trembling with delight suddenly.

120   "I don't want no hep," he said. "I'm doing all right by myself."

Copyright © BookheadEd Learning, LLC

121   Bobby Lee and Hiram came **ambling** back from the woods. Bobby Lee was dragging a yellow shirt with bright blue parrots in it.

122   "Thow me that shirt, Bobby Lee," The Misfit said. The shirt came flying at him and landed on his shoulder and he put it on. The grandmother couldn't name what the shirt reminded her of. "No, lady," The Misfit said while he was buttoning it up, "I found out the crime don't matter. You can do one thing or you can do another, kill a man or take a tire off his car, because sooner or later you're going to forget what it was you done and just be punished for it."

123   The children's mother had begun to make heaving noises as if she couldn't get her breath. "Lady," he asked, "would you and that little girl like to step off yonder with Bobby Lee and Hiram and join your husband?"

124   "Yes, thank you," the mother said faintly. Her left arm dangled helplessly and she was holding the baby, who had gone to sleep, in the other. "Hep that lady up, Hiram," The Misfit said as she struggled to climb out of the ditch, "and Bobby Lee, you hold onto that little girl's hand."

125   "I don't want to hold hands with him," June Star said. "He reminds me of a pig."

126   The fat boy blushed and laughed and caught her by the arm and pulled her off into the woods after Hiram and her mother.

127   Alone with The Misfit, the grandmother found that she had lost her voice. There was not a cloud in the sky nor any sun. There was nothing around her but woods. She wanted to tell him that he must pray. She opened and closed her mouth several times before anything came out. Finally she found herself saying, "Jesus. Jesus," meaning, Jesus will help you, but the way she was saying it, it sounded as if she might be cursing.

128   "Yes'm," The Misfit said as if he agreed. "Jesus thown everything off balance. It was the same case with Him as with me except He hadn't committed any crime and they could prove I had committed one because they had the papers on me. Of course," he said, "they never shown me my papers. That's why I sign myself now. I said long ago, you get you a signature and sign everything you do and keep a copy of it. Then you'll know what you done and you can hold up the crime to the punishment and see do they match and in the end you'll have something to prove you ain't been treated right. I call myself The Misfit," he said, "because I can't make what all I done wrong fit what all I gone through in punishment."

129   There was a piercing scream from the woods, followed closely by a pistol report. "Does it seem right to you, lady, that one is punished a heap and another ain't punished at all?"

130 "Jesus!" the old lady cried. "You've got good blood! I know you wouldn't shoot a lady! I know you come from nice people! Pray! Jesus, you ought not to shoot a lady. I'll give you all the money I've got!"

131 "Lady," The Misfit said, looking beyond her far into the woods, "there never was a body that give the undertaker a tip."

132 There were two more pistol reports and the grandmother raised her head like a parched old turkey hen crying for water and called, "Bailey Boy, Bailey Boy!" as if her heart would break.

133 "Jesus was the only One that ever raised the dead," The Misfit continued, "and He shouldn't have done it. He thown everything off balance. If He did what He said, then it's nothing for you to do but thow away everything and follow Him, and if He didn't, then it's nothing for you to do but enjoy the few minutes you got left the best way you can—by killing somebody or burning down his house or doing some other meanness to him. No pleasure but meanness," he said and his voice had become almost a snarl.

134 "Maybe He didn't raise the dead," the old lady mumbled, not knowing what she was saying and feeling so dizzy that she sank down in the ditch with her legs twisted under her.

135 "I wasn't there so I can't say He didn't," The Misfit said. "I wisht I had of been there," he said, hitting the ground with his fist. "It ain't right I wasn't there because if I had of been there I would of known. Listen lady," he said in a high voice, "if I had of been there I would of known and I wouldn't be like I am now." His voice seemed about to crack and the grandmother's head cleared for an instant. She saw the man's face twisted close to her own as if he were going to cry and she murmured, "Why you're one of my babies. You're one of my own children!" She reached out and touched him on the shoulder. The Misfit sprang back as if a snake had bitten him and shot her three times through the chest. Then he put his gun down on the ground and took off his glasses and began to clean them.

136 Hiram and Bobby Lee returned from the woods and stood over the ditch, looking down at the grandmother who half sat and half lay in a puddle of blood with her legs crossed under her like a child's and her face smiling up at the cloudless sky.

137 Without his glasses, The Misfit's eyes were red-rimmed and pale and defenseless-looking. "Take her off and thow her where you thown the others," he said, picking up the cat that was rubbing itself against his leg.

138 "She was a talker, wasn't she?" Bobby Lee said, sliding down the ditch with a yodel.

139 "She would of been a good woman," The Misfit said, "if it had been somebody there to shoot her every minute of her life."

140 "Some fun!" Bobby Lee said.

141 "Shut up, Bobby Lee," The Misfit said. "It's no real pleasure in life."

"A Good Man Is Hard to Find" from *A Good Man Is Hard to Find and Other Stories* by Flannery O'Connor. Copyright 1953 by Flannery O'Connor; Copyright © Renewed 1981 by Regina O'Connor. Reprinted by Permission of Houghton Mifflin Harcourt Publishing Company. All rights reserved.

Please note that excerpts and passages in the StudySync® library and this workbook are intended as touchstones to generate interest in an author's work. The excerpts and passages do not substitute for the reading of entire texts, and StudySync® strongly recommends that students seek out and purchase the whole literary or informational work in order to experience it as the author intended. Links to online resellers are available in our digital library. In addition, complete works may be ordered through an authorized reseller by filling out and returning to StudySync® the order form enclosed in this workbook.

Reading & Writing Companion   27

First Read

Read "A Good Man Is Hard to Find." After you read, complete the Think Questions below.

☁ THINK QUESTIONS

1. How would you describe the grandmother's general outlook on the world? How does she think and act differently from her son, Bailey, and her grandchildren, John Wesley and June Star?

2. Why does the grandmother recognize the driver of the car? Explain the events in the story leading up to this moment that foreshadow the man's arrival.

3. What is The Misfit's philosophy? How does he see things differently from the grandmother?

4. Based on its context, what do you think the word **jaunty** means? Write your best definition of *jaunty* here, explaining how you determined its meaning.

5. What do you think the word **ambling** means? Look at the context in which the word is used in the story and write your own definition of *ambling* here.

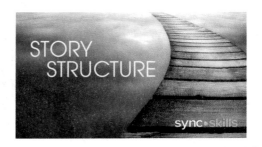

Skill:
Story Structure

Use the Checklist to analyze Story Structure in "A Good Man Is Hard to Find." Refer to the sample student annotations about Story Structure in the text.

••• CHECKLIST FOR STORY STRUCTURE

In order to identify the choices an author makes when structuring specific parts of a text, note the following:

✓ the choices an author makes to organize specific parts of a text such as where to begin and end a story, or whether the ending should be tragic, comic, or inconclusive

✓ the author's use of any literary devices, such as:

- foreshadowing: a way of hinting at what will come later
- flashback: a part of a story that shows something that happened in the past
- pacing: how quickly or slowly the events of a story unfold

✓ how the overall structure of the text contributes to its meaning as well as to its aesthetic impact

- the effect structure has on the reader, such as the creation of suspense through the use of pacing
- the use of flashback to reveal hidden dimensions of a character that affect the theme

To analyze how an author's choices concerning how to structure specific parts of a text contribute to its overall structure and meaning as well as its aesthetic impact, consider the following questions:

✓ How does the author structure the text overall? How does the author structure specific parts of the text?

✓ Does the author incorporate literary elements such as flashback or foreshadowing?

✓ How do these elements affect the overall text structure and the aesthetic impact of the text?

Please note that excerpts and passages in the StudySync® library and this workbook are intended as touchstones to generate interest in an author's work. The excerpts and passages do not substitute for the reading of entire texts, and StudySync® strongly recommends that students seek out and purchase the whole literary or informational work in order to experience it as the author intended. Links to online resellers are available in our digital library. In addition, complete works may be ordered through an authorized reseller by filling out and returning to StudySync® the order form enclosed in this workbook.

Reading & Writing
Companion

29

Skill:
Story Structure

Reread paragraphs 66–72 of "A Good Man Is Hard to Find." Then, using the Checklist on the previous page, answer the multiple-choice questions below.

⟳ YOUR TURN

1. What impact does the author's narration of this scene have on the reader?

    ○ A. It creates comfort, anticipation, and excitement in the reader and sets up the reader for the story's surprise ending.

    ○ B. It creates discomfort, anticipation, and fear in the reader and sets up the reader for the story's eerie, tragic ending.

    ○ C. It creates discomfort, anticipation, and fear in the reader and sets up the reader for the story's happy ending.

    ○ D. It creates comfort, anticipation, and excitement in the reader and sets up the reader for the story's eerie, tragic ending.

2. In this scene, the reader encounters The Misfit. How does the revelation about who he is contribute to the suspense of this scene?

    ○ A. To create suspense, the driver of the car is portrayed with vivid, descriptive details, and the grandmother is described as having a feeling that he is someone she knows, which gives the reader subtle hints about who he is.

    ○ B. To create suspense, the driver of the car is portrayed as a man with glasses that make him look like a scholar, which gives the reader subtle hints about who he is.

    ○ C. To create suspense, the driver of the car is described as getting out of the car and standing by it as the grandmother is screaming that they have had an accident, which gives the reader subtle hints about who he is.

    ○ D. To create suspense, the driver of the car is described as having a gun and no shirt. The grandmother is described as noting that the driver's face is very familiar to her, which gives the reader subtle hints about who he is.

3. The grandmother has a feeling that she recognizes the driver. How does this realization lead to the story's climax?

○ A. The grandmother realizes that she is mistaken and begins to try to persuade the driver not to kill her, and this leads up to the story's climax.

○ B. The grandmother's recognition of the driver makes the reader wonder if he is The Misfit. She then realizes that the man whom she is looking to for help is The Misfit, which is the conflict in the story that leads to the climax.

○ C. The grandmother's recognition of the driver makes the reader wonder if he is The Misfit. She then realizes that the man whom she is looking to for help is The Misfit, and this leads up to the story's climax.

○ D. The grandmother's recognition of the driver makes the reader wonder if the man is related to her. She then realizes that the man whom she is looking to for help is her estranged nephew, and this leads up to the story's climax.

Please note that excerpts and passages in the StudySync® library and this workbook are intended as touchstones to generate interest in an author's work. The excerpts and passages do not substitute for the reading of entire texts, and StudySync® strongly recommends that students seek out and purchase the whole literary or informational work in order to experience it as the author intended. Links to online resellers are available in our digital library. In addition, complete works may be ordered through an authorized reseller by filling out and returning to StudySync® the order form enclosed in this workbook.

Reading & Writing
Companion

31

Skill:
Connotation and Denotation

Use the Checklist to analyze Connotation and Denotation in "A Good Man Is Hard to Find." Refer to the sample student annotation about Connotation and Denotation in the text.

••• CHECKLIST FOR CONNOTATION AND DENOTATION

In order to identify the denotative meanings of words, use the following steps:

✓ first, note unfamiliar words and phrases, key words used to describe important characters, events, and ideas, or words that inspire an emotional reaction

✓ next, determine and note the denotative meanings of words by consulting a reference material such as a dictionary, glossary, or thesaurus

✓ finally, analyze nuances in the meanings of words with similar denotations

To better understand the meanings of words and phrases as they are used in a text, including connotative meanings, use the following questions as a guide:

✓ What is the genre or subject of the text? Based on context, what do you think the meaning of the word is intended to be?

✓ Is your inference the same as or different from the dictionary definition?

✓ Does the word create a positive, negative, or neutral emotion?

✓ What synonyms or alternative phrasings help you describe the connotative meaning of the word?

To determine the meanings of words and phrases as they are used in a text, including connotative meanings, use the following questions as a guide:

✓ What is the denotative meaning of the word? Is that denotative meaning correct in context?

✓ What possible positive, neutral, or negative connotations might the word have, depending on context?

✓ What textual details signal a particular connotation for the word?

Skill:
Connotation and Denotation

Reread paragraphs 49–53 of "A Good Man Is Hard to Find." Then, using the Checklist on the previous page, answer the multiple-choice questions below.

↻ YOUR TURN

1. How does the description of Bailey's jaw as "rigid as a horseshoe" in paragraph 49 affect the reader's understanding of this part of the story?

   ○ A. The description of Bailey's jaw suggests that he is a rigid person but that he is also willing to do things to make his children and mother happy.

   ○ B. The description of Bailey's jaw suggests that he is determined not to stray off course and implies a lack of flexibility.

   ○ C. The description of Bailey's jaw suggests that he is determined not to stray off course and implies that he has opinions that he is unwilling to change.

   ○ D. The description of Bailey's jaw suggests that he is determined to stray off course and implies that although he is flexible he does not want to be told what to do.

2. Which word does not have a negative connotation as used in this excerpt of the text?

   ○ A. desperately
   ○ B. scream
   ○ C. blows
   ○ D. educational

Please note that excerpts and passages in the StudySync® library and this workbook are intended as touchstones to generate interest in an author's work. The excerpts and passages do not substitute for the reading of entire texts, and StudySync® strongly recommends that students seek out and purchase the whole literary or informational work in order to experience it as the author intended. Links to online resellers are available in our digital library. In addition, complete works may be ordered through an authorized reseller by filling out and returning to StudySync® the order form enclosed in this workbook.

Reading & Writing Companion   33

Close Read

Reread "A Good Man Is Hard to Find." As you reread, complete the Skills Focus questions below. Then use your answers and annotations from the questions to help you complete the Write activity.

◎ SKILLS FOCUS

1. Identify the attitude the children have towards their grandmother. Find examples of words with negative connotations that reveal the kids' tone.

2. In what ways does the grandmother manipulate her family members? How do her manipulations contribute to the story's tragic ending?

3. How does the scene with Red Sam and his wife contribute to the overall structure of the story? Identify evidence from the text to support your answer.

4. How does the ending of the story contribute to its overall meaning? Identify evidence from the text to support your answer.

5. How does the grandmother's perspective change over the course of the story? Find evidence to support your answer.

✎ WRITE

LITERARY ANALYSIS: Analyze the way the short story "A Good Man Is Hard to Find" uses story structure to express and contribute to the text's overall meaning. Be sure to include the most relevant evidence from the text to support your response.

The Marshall Plan Speech

ARGUMENTATIVE TEXT
George Marshall
1947

Introduction

In 1947, Europe was reeling from the devastation of World War II. Governments lacked funds to rebuild roads, bridges, and factories. People were sick and starving. At the same time, tensions were mounting between the Soviet Union and the United States. Although the superpowers had fought together against Nazi Germany during the war, the United States feared Russian expansion and the spread of Communism. The same year, Secretary of State George Marshall, a retired five-star general appointed to his position by President Truman, delivered a brief commencement address at Harvard University that would have an enormous impact on Europe's recovery. In the four years following Marshall's speech, the United States sent billions of dollars in assistance to European nations, helping countries rebuild infrastructure and restore financial institutions.

"Any government which maneuvers to block the recovery of other countries cannot expect help from us."

Stalingrad, USSR. Stalingrad during a German air raid in the Battle of Stalingrad on the Eastern Front of World War II. The battle marked a turning point in the war, and paved the way for the Red Army's advance on Berlin in 1945.

Warsaw in ruins at the end of World War II

Rebuilding Dresden
Women form a human chain to carry bricks used in the reconstruction of Dresden, March 1946, after Allied bombing had destroyed the city in February 1945. The steeple of the wrecked Roman Catholic cathedral can be seen in the background.

Skill:
Informational Text
Structure

The speaker, George Marshall, begins by introducing a problem, so this is likely a problem-solution structure. He uses words that suggest that the problem is very serious and that people will struggle to understand the problem's complexity.

1   I need not tell you gentlemen that the world situation is very serious. That must be apparent to all intelligent people. I think one difficulty is that the problem is one of such enormous complexity that the very mass of facts presented to the public by press and radio make it **exceedingly** difficult for the man in the street to reach a clear appraisement of the situation. Furthermore, the people of this country are distant from the troubled areas of the earth and it is hard for them to comprehend the plight and consequent reactions of the long-suffering peoples, and the effect of those reactions on their governments in connection with our efforts to promote peace in the world.

2   In considering the requirements for the rehabilitation of Europe the physical loss of life, the visible destruction of cities, factories, mines and railroads was correctly estimated, but it has become obvious during recent months that this visible destruction was probably less serious than the dislocation of the entire fabric of European economy. For the past ten years conditions have been highly abnormal. The feverish preparation for war and the more feverish maintenance of the war effort engulfed all aspects of national economies. Machinery has fallen into disrepair or is entirely obsolete. Under the **arbitrary** and destructive Nazi rule, virtually every possible enterprise was geared into the German war machine. Long-standing commercial ties, private institutions, banks, insurance companies and shipping companies disappeared, through loss of capital, absorption through nationalization or by simple destruction. In many countries, confidence in the local currency has been severely shaken. The breakdown of the business structure of Europe during the war was complete. Recovery has been seriously retarded by the fact that two years after the close of hostilities a peace settlement with Germany and Austria has not been agreed upon. But even given a more prompt solution of these difficult problems, the rehabilitation of the economic structure of Europe quite evidently will require a much longer time and greater effort than had been foreseen.

Skill: Word
Patterns and
Relationships

The words producing and produce have the same base word, but producing is functioning as a verb and produce as a noun. I can infer that farm produce is produced by farmers and is what they sell.

3   There is a phase of this matter which is both interesting and serious. The farmer has always produced the foodstuffs to exchange with the city dweller for the other necessities of life. This division of labor is the basis of modern civilization. At the present time it is threatened with breakdown. The town and city industries are not producing **adequate** goods to exchange with the food-producing farmer. Raw materials and fuel are in short supply. Machinery is lacking or worn out. The farmer or the peasant cannot find the goods for sale which he desires to purchase. So the sale of his farm produce for money which he cannot use seems to him an unprofitable transaction. He, therefore, has withdrawn many fields from crop cultivation and is using them for grazing. He feeds more grain to stock and finds for himself and his family an ample supply of food, however short he may be on clothing and the other ordinary gadgets of civilization. Meanwhile people in the cities are short of food and

fuel. So the governments are forced to use their foreign money and credits to procure these necessities abroad. This process exhausts funds which are urgently needed for reconstruction. Thus a very serious situation is rapidly developing which bodes no good for the world. The modern system of the division of labor upon which the exchange of products is based is in danger of breaking down.

4   The truth of the matter is that Europe's requirements for the next three or four years of foreign food and other essential products—principally from America—are so much greater than her present ability to pay that she must have substantial additional help, or face economic, social and political **deterioration** of a very grave character.

5   The remedy lies in breaking the vicious circle and restoring the confidence of the European people in the economic future of their own countries and of Europe as a whole. The manufacturer and the farmer throughout wide areas must be able and willing to exchange their products for currencies the continuing value of which is not open to question.

6   Aside from the demoralizing effect on the world at large and the possibilities of disturbances arising as a result of the desperation of the people concerned, the consequences to the economy of the United States should be apparent to all. It is logical that the United States should do whatever it is able to do to assist in the return of normal economic health in the world, without which there can be no political stability and no assured peace. Our policy is directed not against any country or doctrine but against hunger, poverty, desperation and chaos. Its purpose should be the revival of a working economy in the world so as to permit the emergence of political and social conditions in which free institutions can exist. Such assistance, I am convinced, must not be on a piece-meal basis as various crises develop. Any assistance that this Government may **render** in the future should provide a cure rather than a mere palliative. Any government that is willing to assist in the task of recovery will find full cooperation, I am sure, on the part of the United States Government. Any government which maneuvers to block the recovery of other countries cannot expect help from us. Furthermore, governments, political parties or groups which seek to perpetuate human misery in order to profit therefrom politically or otherwise will encounter the opposition of the United States.

7   It is already evident that, before the United States Government can proceed much further in its efforts to **alleviate** the situation and help start the European world on its way to recovery, there must be some agreement among the countries of Europe as to the requirements of the situation and the part those countries themselves will take in order to give proper effect to whatever action might be undertaken by this Government. It would be neither fitting nor efficacious for this Government to undertake to draw up **unilaterally** a

Skill: Author's Purpose and Point of View

Words like demoralizing, consequences, apparent, and logical strengthen Marshall's claim that inaction will prevent any chance of peace. These words support his argument, establish credibility, and appeal to his audience.

NOTES

program designed to place Europe on its feet economically. This is the business of the Europeans. The initiative, I think, must come from Europe. The role of this country should consist of friendly aid in the drafting of a European program and of later support of such a program so far as it may be practical for U.S. to do so. The program should be a joint one, agreed to by a number, if not all European nations.

8   An essential part of any successful action on the part of the United States is an understanding on the part of the people of America of the character of the problem and the remedies to be applied. Political passion and prejudice should have no part. With foresight, and a willingness on the part of our people to face up to the vast responsibility which history has clearly placed upon our country, the difficulties I have outlined can and will be overcome.

First Read

Read "The Marshall Plan Speech." After you read, complete the Think Questions below.

☁ THINK QUESTIONS

1. Speakers often try to persuade an audience to like them. They do this in order to get a point across. How does Marshall attempt to win over his audience in the opening paragraphs of his speech?

2. What are some of the reasons Marshall mentions in paragraph 2 for the economic instability in Europe?

3. What role does Marshall think the United States should play in the recovery of Europe?

4. Based on context clues in paragraph 7, what do you think the word **alleviate** means? Write your best definition of *alleviate* here, explaining how you arrived at its meaning.

5. The Latin word *lateralis* means "belonging to the side." With this in mind and using context from the text, try to infer the meaning of the word **unilaterally** as it is used in paragraph 7. Write your best definition of the word here.

Please note that excerpts and passages in the StudySync® library and this workbook are intended as touchstones to generate interest in an author's work. The excerpts and passages do not substitute for the reading of entire texts, and StudySync® strongly recommends that students seek out and purchase the whole literary or informational work in order to experience it as the author intended. Links to online resellers are available in our digital library. In addition, complete works may be ordered through an authorized reseller by filling out and returning to StudySync® the order form enclosed in this workbook.

Reading & Writing Companion   41

Skill: Author's Purpose and Point of View

Use the Checklist to analyze Author's Purpose and Point of View in "The Marshall Plan Speech." Refer to the sample student annotation about Author's Purpose and Point of View in the text.

••• CHECKLIST FOR AUTHOR'S PURPOSE AND POINT OF VIEW

In order to identify author's purpose and point of view, note the following:

- ✓ whether the writer is attempting to establish trust by citing his or her experience or education

- ✓ whether the evidence the author provides is convincing and the argument or position is logical

- ✓ what words and phrases the author uses to appeal to the emotions

- ✓ the author's use of rhetoric, or the art of speaking and writing persuasively, such as the use of repetition to drive home a point, as well as allusion and alliteration

- ✓ the author's use of rhetoric to contribute to the power, persuasiveness, or beauty of the text

To determine the author's purpose and point of view, consider the following questions:

- ✓ How does the author try to convince me that he or she has something valid and important for me to read?

- ✓ What words or phrases express emotion or invite an emotional response? How or why are they effective or ineffective?

- ✓ What words and phrases contribute to the power, persuasiveness, or beauty of the text? Is the author's use of rhetoric successful? Why or why not?

Skill: Author's Purpose and Point of View

Reread paragraphs 6 and 7 of "The Marshall Plan Speech." Then, using the Checklist on the previous page, answer the multiple-choice questions below.

↻ YOUR TURN

1. This question has two parts. First, answer Part A. Then, answer Part B.

   Part A: Based on Marshall's remarks in paragraph 6, the reader can conclude that Marshall's point of view is that it is imperative—

   ○ A. to proceed one step at a time.
   ○ B. that all countries receive help from the United States.
   ○ C. to encourage freedom throughout the world.
   ○ D. that America negotiate peace in Europe.

   Part B: Which line from the passage best supports your answer in Part A?

   ○ A. "Any government that is willing to assist in the task of recovery will find full cooperation, I am sure, on the part of the United States Government."
   ○ B. "Any government which maneuvers to block the recovery of other countries cannot expect help from us."
   ○ C. "Our policy is directed not against any country or doctrine but against hunger, poverty, desperation and chaos."
   ○ D. "Its purpose should be the revival of a working economy in the world so as to permit the emergence of political and social conditions in which free institutions can exist."

2. What is Marshall's purpose in paragraph 7?

   ○ A. He wants countries in Europe to reach an agreement before receiving help.
   ○ B. He is stating that the United States Government is ready to begin help immediately.
   ○ C. He wants to clarify the role of the countries involved in an agreement.
   ○ D. He is emphasizing the urgency in coming to an agreement.

Please note that excerpts and passages in the StudySync® library and this workbook are intended as touchstones to generate interest in an author's work. The excerpts and passages do not substitute for the reading of entire texts, and StudySync® strongly recommends that students seek out and purchase the whole literary or informational work in order to experience it as the author intended. Links to online resellers are available in our digital library. In addition, complete works may be ordered through an authorized reseller by filling out and returning to StudySync® the order form enclosed in this workbook.

Reading & Writing Companion

43

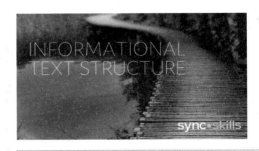

Skill:
Informational Text Structure

Use the Checklist to analyze Informational Text Structure in "The Marshall Plan Speech." Refer to the sample student annotation about Informational Text Structure in the text.

••• CHECKLIST FOR INFORMATIONAL TEXT STRUCTURE

In order to determine the structure an author uses in his or her writing, note the following:

- ✓ where the author introduces and clarifies his or her argument

- ✓ sentences and paragraphs that reveal the text structure the author uses to frame the argument

- ✓ whether the text structure is effective in presenting all sides of the argument, and makes his or her points clear, convincing, and engaging

To analyze and evaluate the effectiveness of the structure an author uses in his or her writing, including whether the structure makes points clear, convincing, and engaging, consider the following questions:

- ✓ Did I have to read a particular sentence or paragraph over again? Where?

- ✓ Did I find myself distracted or uninterested while reading the text? When?

- ✓ Did the structure the author used make his or her points clear, convincing, and engaging? Why or why not?

- ✓ Was the author's exposition or argument effective? Why or why not?

- ✓ In what ways did the structure of the text enhance my understanding of the argument and its development?

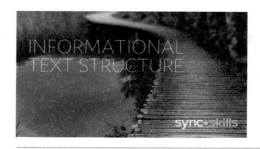

Skill:
Informational Text Structure

Reread paragraphs 7 and 8 of "The Marshall Plan Speech." Then, using the Checklist on the previous page, answer the multiple-choice questions below.

⟳ YOUR TURN

1. This question has two parts. First, answer Part A. Then, answer Part B.

    Part A: What is the purpose of paragraph 7 in relation to the overall structure of the text?

    ○ A. to ensure Americans that the U.S. government is prepared to do whatever it takes to aid in Europe's recovery

    ○ B. to ensure the American people that the U.S. involvement will be to provide programs to support Europe's economic recovery

    ○ C. to assure Americans that U.S. involvement will be limited as well as make it clear that he believes that Europe's economic recovery is their responsibility

    ○ D. to persuade the American people to give money to aid in Europe's recovery.

    Part B: Which line from the passage best supports your answer in Part A?

    ○ A. "The role of this country should consist of friendly aid in the drafting of a European program and of later support of such a program so far as it may be practical for us to do so."

    ○ B. "The program should be a joint one, agreed to by a number, if not all European nations."

    ○ C. "The initiative, I think, must come from Europe."

    ○ D. "It would be neither fitting nor efficacious for this Government to undertake to draw up unilaterally a program designed to place Europe on its feet economically. This is the business of the Europeans."

Please note that excerpts and passages in the StudySync® library and this workbook are intended as touchstones to generate interest in an author's work. The excerpts and passages do not substitute for the reading of entire texts, and StudySync® strongly recommends that students seek out and purchase the whole literary or informational work in order to experience it as the author intended. Links to online resellers are available in our digital library. In addition, complete works may be ordered through an authorized reseller by filling out and returning to StudySync® the order form enclosed in this workbook.

Reading & Writing Companion

45

2. How does the final paragraph of the speech serve to make the speech more convincing?

    ○ A. It appeals to the character of the American people and explains the solutions that will be applied.

    ○ B. It appeals to the morality of the American people and suggests that Americans need to keep passion and prejudice out of this.

    ○ C. It appeals to the common sense of the American people and explains that they should understand the solutions being proposed.

    ○ D. It appeals to a sense of duty that Americans have to be a part of his proposed solution and makes it clear that the struggles they are facing will be overcome.

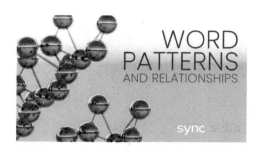

Skill: Word Patterns and Relationships

Use the Checklist to analyze Word Patterns and Relationships in "The Marshall Plan Speech." Refer to the sample student annotation about Word Patterns and Relationships in the text.

••• CHECKLIST FOR WORD PATTERNS AND RELATIONSHIPS

In order to identify patterns of word changes to indicate different meanings or parts of speech, do the following:

- ✓ determine the word's part of speech

- ✓ use context clues to make a preliminary determination of the meaning of the word

- ✓ identify other words in the text or that you are familiar with that share a base word with the word in question and may have a similar meaning

- ✓ use knowledge of common root words, prefixes, and suffixes to determine a word's part of speech or meaning

- ✓ consult a dictionary to verify your preliminary determination of the meanings and parts of speech

- ✓ be sure to read all the definitions, and then decide which definition, form, and part of speech makes sense within the context of the text

To identify and correctly use patterns of word changes that indicate different meanings or parts of speech, consider the following questions:

- ✓ What is the intended meaning of the word?

- ✓ Do I know that this word form is the correct part of speech? Do I understand the word patterns for this particular word?

- ✓ When I consult a dictionary, can I confirm that the meaning I have determined for this word is correct? Do I know how to use it correctly?

Please note that excerpts and passages in the StudySync® library and this workbook are intended as touchstones to generate interest in an author's work. The excerpts and passages do not substitute for the reading of entire texts, and StudySync® strongly recommends that students seek out and purchase the whole literary or informational work in order to experience it as the author intended. Links to online resellers are available in our digital library. In addition, complete works may be ordered through an authorized reseller by filling out and returning to StudySync® the order form enclosed in this workbook.

Reading & Writing Companion   47

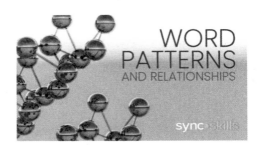

Skill: Word Patterns and Relationships

Reread paragraphs 6 and 7 of "The Marshall Plan Speech." Then, using the Checklist on the previous page, answer the multiple-choice questions below.

↻ YOUR TURN

1. What is the relationship between the words *economy* and *economic*?

    ○ A. They have the same root word, and they are both used as nouns in the sentence. Both have to do with finances.

    ○ B. They have the same root word, but *economy* is a noun and *economic* is an adjective. Both have to do with finances.

    ○ C. They have the same root word, and *economy* is a noun and *economic* is an adverb. Both have to do with finances.

    ○ D. They do not share the same root word as the word endings for each are different.

2. Using your answer from question 1, what can you infer about the word part and meaning of the word *economically* in paragraph 7?

    ○ A. It is an adjective used to describe the way in which the United States will support European countries with money.

    ○ B. It is a verb used to show the action that the European countries will take to support European countries.

    ○ C. It is an adverb used to describe the way in which the United States will support European countries with money.

    ○ D. It is an adverb used to describe the way in which business will operate in Europe.

The Marshall Plan Speech

Close Read

Reread "The Marshall Plan Speech." As you reread, complete the Skills Focus questions below. Then use your answers and annotations from the questions to help you complete the Write activity.

◎ SKILLS FOCUS

1. Identify a passage in which Marshall addresses his audience directly. Analyze how he connects his message to his audience.

2. Identify two words that share the same base word in paragraph 2. Identify the part of speech of each word and explain the relationship between their meanings.

3. Find a passage in which Marshall reinforces his message by pointing out that the recovery in Europe will take longer than people expected. Analyze his purpose for including this statement.

4. Identify a portion of the speech in which Marshall describes the problem he wants to solve. How does his use of structure in describing this problem help make his plea for support more convincing?

5. In this speech, Marshall describes his plan for helping Europe rebuild. How do you think Marshall would measure the success of his plan? Support your response with evidence from the text.

✎ WRITE

RHETORICAL ANALYSIS: The Marshall Plan Speech was a rallying cry to America, a call to help Europe rebuild after the devastation of World War II. Write a rhetorical analysis in which you determine how Marshall structures his argument to Americans. Then, evaluate the effectiveness of this structure, as well as the rhetoric and reasoning Marshall uses to persuade his audience of his point of view. Use textual evidence and original commentary to support your response.

Please note that excerpts and passages in the StudySync® library and this workbook are intended as touchstones to generate interest in an author's work. The excerpts and passages do not substitute for the reading of entire texts, and StudySync® strongly recommends that students seek out and purchase the whole literary or informational work in order to experience it as the author intended. Links to online resellers are available in our digital library. In addition, complete works may be ordered through an authorized reseller by filling out and returning to StudySync® the order form enclosed in this workbook.

Reading & Writing Companion   49

On the Road

FICTION
Jack Kerouac
1957

Introduction

Jack Kerouac (1922–1969) was a poet and novelist often celebrated as the voice of a generation. Along with his friends Allen Ginsberg and William S. Burroughs, Kerouac was a key figure in what is remembered as the "Beat Generation"—a literary movement that endeavored to give literature a freedom to stray from academics and rigid structure. This excerpt is from Kerouac's most widely read work, *On the Road*, a semi-autobiographical novel based on his own travels. As readers will come to witness in this excerpt, the beginning of a journey can often

"All I could see were smoky trees and dismal wilderness rising to the skies."

Copyright © BookheadEd Learning, LLC

NOTES

1   In the month of July 1947, having saved about fifty dollars from old veteran benefits, I was ready to go to the West Coast. My friend Remi Boncœur had written me a letter from San Francisco, saying I should come and ship out with him on an around-the-world liner. He swore he could get me into the engine room. I wrote back and said I'd be satisfied with any old freighter so long as I could take a few long Pacific trips and come back with enough money to support myself in my aunt's house while I finished my book. He said he had a shack in Mill City and I would have all the time in the world to write there while we went through the **rigmarole** of getting the ship. He was living with a girl called Lee Ann; he said she was a marvelous cook and everything would jump. Remi was an old prep-school friend, a Frenchman brought up in Paris and a really mad guy—I didn't know how mad at this time. So he expected me to arrive in ten days. My aunt was all in accord with my trip to the West; she said it would do me good, I'd been working so hard all winter and staying in too much; she even didn't complain when I told her I'd have to hitchhike some. All she wanted was for me to come back in one piece. So, leaving my big half-manuscript sitting on top of my desk, and folding back my comfortable home sheets for the last time one morning, I left with my canvas bag in which a few fundamental things were packed and took off for the Pacific Ocean with the fifty dollars in my pocket.

2   I'd been poring over maps of the United States in Paterson for months, even reading books about the pioneers and **savoring** names like Platte and Cimarron and so on, and on the roadmap was one long red line called Route 6 that led from the tip of Cape Cod clear to Ely, Nevada, and there dipped down to Los Angeles. I'll just stay on 6 all the way to Ely, I said to myself and confidently started. To get to 6 I had to go up to Bear Mountain. Filled with dreams of what I'd do in Chicago, in Denver, and then finally in San Fran, I took the Seventh Avenue subway to the end of the line at 242nd Street, and there took a trolley into Yonkers; in downtown Yonkers I transferred to an outgoing trolley and went to the city limits on the east bank of the Hudson River. If you drop a rose in the Hudson River at its mysterious source in the Adirondacks, think of all the places it journeys by as it goes out to sea forever—think of that wonderful Hudson Valley. I started hitching up the thing. Five scattered rides took me to the desired Bear Mountain Bridge, where Route 6 arched in from New England. It began to

rain in **torrents** when I was let off there. It was mountainous. Route 6 came over the river, wound around a traffic circle, and disappeared into the wilderness. Not only was there no traffic but the rain came down in buckets and I had no shelter. I had to run under some pines to take cover; this did no good; I began crying and swearing and socking myself on the head for being such a damn fool. I was forty miles north of New York; all the way up I'd been worried about the fact that on this, my big opening day, I was only moving north instead of the so-longed-for west. Now I was stuck on my northernmost hangup. I ran a quarter-mile to an abandoned cute English-style filling station and stood under the dripping eaves. High up over my head the great hairy Bear Mountain sent down thunderclaps that put the fear of God in me. All I could see were smoky trees and dismal wilderness rising to the skies. "What the hell am I doing up here?" I cursed, I cried for Chicago. "Even now they're all having a big time, they're doing this, I'm not there, when will I get there!"—and so on. Finally a car stopped at the empty filling station; the man and the two women in it wanted to study a map. I stepped right up and gestured in the rain; they consulted; I looked like a maniac, of course, with my hair all wet, my shoes sopping. My shoes, damn fool that I am, were Mexican huaraches, plantlike **sieves** not fit for the rainy night of America and the raw road night. But the people let me in and rode me north to Newburgh, which I accepted as a better alternative than being trapped in the Bear Mountain wilderness all night. "Besides," said the man, "there's no traffic passes through 6. If you want to go to Chicago you'd do better going across the Holland Tunnel in New York and head for Pittsburgh," and I knew he was right. It was my dream that screwed up, the stupid hearthside idea that it would be wonderful to follow one great red line across America instead of trying various roads and routes.

3   In Newburgh it had stopped raining. I walked down to the river, and I had to ride back to New York in a bus with a **delegation** of schoolteachers coming back from a weekend in the mountains—chatter-chatter blah-blah, and me swearing for all the time and the money I'd wasted, and telling myself, I wanted to go west and here I've been all day and into the night going up and down, north and south, like something that can't get started. And I swore I'd be in Chicago tomorrow, and made sure of that, taking a bus to Chicago, spending most of my money, and didn't give a damn, just as long as I'd be in Chicago tomorrow.

Excerpted from *On the Road* by Jack Kerouac, published by Penguin.

WRITE

PERSONAL NARRATIVE: *On the Road* relates the tale of a protagonist who sets a goal for his trip to the West Coast but is often diverted from his original plans and needs to adjust; sometimes he considers diversions a burden, other times he views them as a plus. Consider the ideas discussed in the texts of this unit, as well as your own experiences. Then write a personal narrative that describes a time you set a goal and had to adjust your plans to succeed. Be sure to include thoughtful details to convey a vivid picture of your experiences.

Please note that excerpts and passages in the StudySync® library and this workbook are intended as touchstones to generate interest in an author's work. The excerpts and passages do not substitute for the reading of entire texts, and StudySync® strongly recommends that students seek out and purchase the whole literary or informational work in order to experience it as the author intended. Links to online resellers are available in our digital library. In addition, complete works may be ordered through an authorized reseller by filling out and returning to StudySync® the order form enclosed in this workbook.

Reading & Writing Companion   **53**

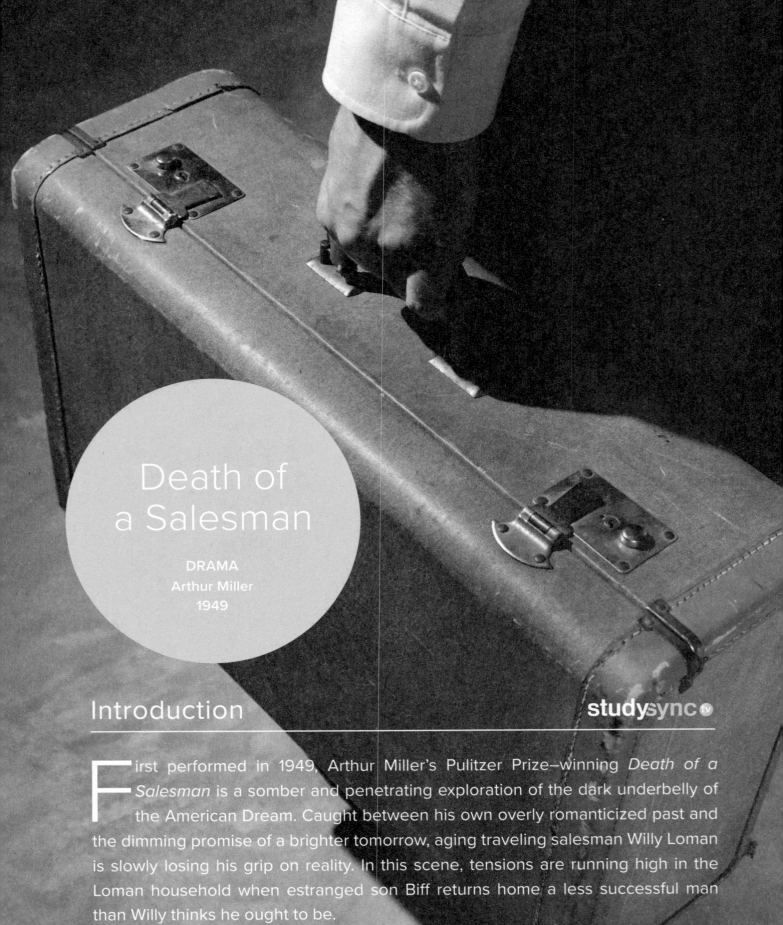

Death of a Salesman

DRAMA
Arthur Miller
1949

Introduction

First performed in 1949, Arthur Miller's Pulitzer Prize–winning *Death of a Salesman* is a somber and penetrating exploration of the dark underbelly of the American Dream. Caught between his own overly romanticized past and the dimming promise of a brighter tomorrow, aging traveling salesman Willy Loman is slowly losing his grip on reality. In this scene, tensions are running high in the Loman household when estranged son Biff returns home a less successful man than Willy thinks he ought to be.

"No, no, some people—some people accomplish something."

from ACT ONE

1 WILLY: Figure it out. Work a lifetime to pay off a house. You finally own it, and there's nobody to live in it.

2 LINDA: Well, dear, life is a casting off. It's always that way.

3 WILLY: No, no, some people—some people accomplish something. Did Biff say anything after I went this morning?

4 LINDA: You shouldn't have criticised him, Willy, especially after he just got off the train. You mustn't lose your temper with him.

5 WILLY: When the hell did I lose my temper? I simply asked him if he was making any money. Is that a criticism?

6 LINDA: But, dear, how could he make any money?

7 WILLY (worried and angered): There's such an **undercurrent** in him. He became a moody man. Did he apologize when I left this morning?

8 LINDA: He was **crestfallen**, Willy. You know how he admires you. I think if he finds himself, then you'll both be happier and not fight any more.

9 WILLY: How can he find himself on a farm? Is that a life? A farmhand? In the beginning, when he was young, I thought, well, a young man, it's good for him to **tramp** around, take a lot of different jobs. But it's more than ten years now and he has yet to make thirty-five dollars a week!

10 LINDA: He's finding himself, Willy.

11 WILLY: Not finding yourself at the age of thirty-four is a disgrace!

12 LINDA: Shh!

13 WILLY: The trouble is he's lazy, goddammit!

Please note that excerpts and passages in the StudySync® library and this workbook are intended as touchstones to generate interest in an author's work. The excerpts and passages do not substitute for the reading of entire texts, and StudySync® strongly recommends that students seek out and purchase the whole literary or informational work in order to experience it as the author intended. Links to online resellers are available in our digital library. In addition, complete works may be ordered through an authorized reseller by filling out and returning to StudySync® the order form enclosed in this workbook.

Reading & Writing
Companion

55

14 LINDA: Willy, please!

15 WILLY: Biff is a lazy bum!

16 LINDA: They're sleeping. Get something to eat. Go on down.

17 WILLY: Why did he come home? I would like to know what brought him home.

18 LINDA: I don't know. I think he's still lost, Willy. I think he's very lost.

19 WILLY: Biff Loman is lost. In the greatest country in the world a young man with such—personal attractiveness, gets lost. And such a hard worker. There's one thing about Biff—he's not lazy.

20 LINDA: Never.

21 WILLY (with pity and **resolve**): I'll see him in the morning; I'll have a nice talk with him. I'll get him a job selling. He could be big in no time. My God! Remember how they used to follow him around in high school? When he smiled at one of them their faces lit up. When he walked down the street . . . (He loses himself in **reminiscences**.)

22 LINDA (trying to bring him out of it): Willy, dear, I got a new kind of American-type cheese today. It's whipped.

23 WILLY: Why do you get American when I like Swiss?

24 LINDA: I just thought you'd like a change . . .

25 WILLY: I don't want a change! I want Swiss cheese. Why am I always being contradicted?

26 LINDA (with a covering laugh): I thought it would be a surprise.

Excerpted from *Death of a Salesman* by Arthur Miller, published by the Penguin Group.

✏ WRITE

PERSONAL RESPONSE: This excerpt focuses on Willy's rigid idea of success and the way it conflicts with his son Biff's actions. Consider the ideas you have read in this text, as well as individuals you admire. In your opinion, what makes a person successful? How do our definitions of success inform our goals? Provide evidence from the text to support your response.

A Raisin in the Sun

DRAMA
Lorraine Hansberry
1959

Introduction

studysync TV

Set in the years after World War II, *A Raisin in the Sun* is an award-winning play by Lorraine Hansberry (1930–1965) about the Youngers, a fictional black family in Chicago struggling to keep things together during difficult financial times. In this excerpt from the third act of the play, son Walter has made a bad business decision and has lost the insurance money the family received from their father's death. He now comes up with a scheme to get some of the money back—but at what price?

"There is always something left to love. And if you ain't learned that you ain't learned nothing."

Note: The text you are about to read contains offensive language. Remember to be mindful of the thoughts and feelings of your peers as you read and discuss this text. Please consult your teacher for additional guidance and support.

Skill: Dramatic Elements and Structure

Walter explains what happened earlier in the day, establishing context. Walter's behavior, relayed through stage directions, is flippant. Ruth's action and dialogue build tension, advancing the plot into the rising action.

from Act III

1 RUTH: What did you call that man for, Walter Lee?

2 WALTER: Called him to tell him to come on over to the show. Gonna put on a show for the man. Just what he wants to see. You see, Mama, the man came here today and he told us that them people out there where you want us to move—well they so upset they willing to pay us not to move! *[He laughs.]* And—and oh, Mama you would have been proud of the way me and Ruth and Bennie acted. We told him to get out . . . . Lord have mercy! We told the man to get out! Oh, we was some proud folks this afternoon, yeah. *[He lights a cigarette.]* We were still full of that old-time stuff . . . .

3 RUTH (Walter's wife) *[coming toward him slowly]*: You talking 'bout taking them people's money to keep us from moving in that house?

4 WALTER: I ain't just talking 'bout it baby—I'm telling you that's what's going to happen!

5 BENEATHA (Walter's sister): Oh, God! Where is the bottom! Where is the real honest-to-God bottom so he can't go any farther!

6 WALTER: See—that's the old stuff. You and that boy was here today. You all want everybody to carry a flag and a spear and sing some marching songs, huh? You wanna spend your life looking into things and trying to find the right and wrong part, huh? Yeah. You know what's going to happen to that boy someday—he'll find himself sitting in a dungeon, locked in forever—and the takers will have the key! Forget it, baby! There ain't no causes—there ain't nothing but taking in this world, and he who takes most is smartest—and it don't make a damn bit of difference *how*.

7 MAMA: You making something inside me cry, son. Some awful pain inside me.

8 WALTER: Don't cry, Mama. Understand. That white man is going to walk in that door able to write checks for more money than we ever had. It's important to him and I'm going to help him . . . I'm going to put on the show, Mama.

9 MAMA: Son—I come from five generations of people who was slaves and **sharecroppers**—but ain't nobody in my family never let nobody pay 'em no money that was a way of telling us we weren't fit to walk the earth. We ain't never been that poor. [*Raising her eyes and looking at him*] We ain't never been that—dead inside.

10 BENEATHA: Well—we are dead now. All the talk about dreams and sunlight that goes on in this house. It's all dead now.

11 WALTER: What's the matter with you all! I didn't make this world! It was give to me this way! Hell, yes, I want me some yachts someday! Yes, I want to hang some real pearls 'round my wife's neck. Ain't she supposed to wear no pearls? Somebody tell me—tell me, who decides which women is suppose to wear pearls in this world. I tell you I am a *man*—and I think my wife should wear some pearls in this world!

12 [*This last line hangs a good while and WALTER begins to move about the room. The word "Man" has penetrated his consciousness; he mumbles it to himself repeatedly between strange agitated pauses as he moves about.*]

13 MAMA: Baby, how you going to feel on the inside?

14 WALTER: Fine! . . . Going to feel fine . . . a man . . .

15 MAMA: You won't have nothing left then, Walter Lee.

16 WALTER [*coming to her*]: I'm going to feel fine, Mama. I'm going to look that son-of-a-bitch in the eyes and say—[*He falters.*]—and say, "All right, Mr. Lindner—[*He falters even more.*]—that's *your* neighborhood out there! You got the right to keep it like you want! You got the right to have it like you want! Just write the check and—the house is yours." And—and I am going to say— [*His voice almost breaks.*] "And you—you people just put the money in my hand and you won't have to live next to this bunch of stinking n------!"

17 . . . And maybe I'll just get down on my black knees . . . [*He does so,* RUTH *and* BENNIE *and* MAMA *watch him in frozen horror.*] "Captain, Mistuh, Bossman— [**groveling** *and grinning and wringing his hands in profoundly anguished imitation of the slow-witted movie stereotype*] Oh, yassuh boss! Yasssssuh! Great white—[*Voice breaking, he forces himself to go on.*]—Father, just gi' ussen de money, fo' God's sake, and we's—we's ain't gwine come out deh and dirty up yo' white folks neighborhood . . ." [*He breaks down completely.*] And I'll feel fine! Fine! FINE! [*He gets up and goes into the bedroom.*]

NOTES

Skill: Dramatic Elements and Structure

Walter's words seem defiant, but the pauses and repetition in his speech, combined with the stage directions, undermine what he is saying. Walter's conscience is breaking through his rant, marking the beginning of the climax.

Please note that excerpts and passages in the StudySync® library and this workbook are intended as touchstones to generate interest in an author's work. The excerpts and passages do not substitute for the reading of entire texts, and StudySync® strongly recommends that students seek out and purchase the whole literary or informational work in order to experience it as the author intended. Links to online resellers are available in our digital library. In addition, complete works may be ordered through an authorized reseller by filling out and returning to StudySync® the order form enclosed in this workbook.

Reading & Writing Companion **59**

NOTES

Skill:
Theme

The characters' dialogue in response to Walter's decision creates conflict. Mama reminds Beneatha about the value of unconditional love. This reveals one of the play's themes about the importance of family.

18   BENEATHA: That is not a man. That is nothing but a toothless rat.

19   MAMA: Yes—death done come in this here house. [*She is nodding, slowly,* ***reflectively***.] Done come walking in my house on the lips of my children. You what supposed to be my beginning again. You—what supposed to be my harvest. [*to* BENEATHA] You—you mourning your brother?

20   BENEATHA: He's no brother of mine.

21   MAMA: What you say?

22   BENEATHA: I said that that individual in that room is no brother of mine.

23   MAMA: That's what I thought you said. You feeling like you better than he is today?

24   [BENEATHA *does not answer.*]

25   MAMA: Yes? What you tell him a minute ago? That he wasn't a man? Yes? You give him up for me? You done wrote his **epitaph** too—like the rest of the world? Well who give you the privilege?

26   BENEATHA: Be on my side for once! You saw what he just did, Mama! You saw him—down on his knees. Wasn't it you who taught me—to **despise** any man who would do that? Do what he's going to do?

27   MAMA: Yes—I taught you that. Me and your daddy. But I thought I taught you something else too . . . I thought I taught you to love him.

28   BENEATHA: Love him? There is nothing left to love.

29   MAMA: There is always something left to love. And if you ain't learned that you ain't learned nothing. [*looking at her*] Have you cried for that boy today? I don't mean for yourself and for the family 'cause we lost the money. I mean for him; what he been through and what it done to him. Child, when do you think is the time to love somebody the most; when they done good and made things easy for everybody? Well then, you ain't through learning—because that ain't the time at all. It's when he's at his lowest and can't believe in hisself 'cause the world done whipped him so! When you starts measuring somebody, measure him right, child, measure him right. Make sure you done taken into account what hills and valleys he come through before he got to wherever he is.

Excerpted from *A Raisin in the Sun* by Lorraine Hansberry, published by Vintage Books.

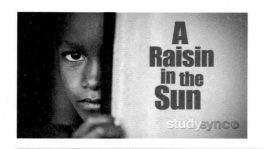

First Read

Read *A Raisin in the Sun*. After you read, complete the Think Questions below.

☁ THINK QUESTIONS

1. Based on the text, what can you infer about Mr. Lindner's motivations for paying Walter and his family not to move?

2. How does Walter define manhood? Cite specific quotes or passages from the text to support your answer.

3. Why is Mama upset at Beneatha? Refer to specific moments in the text in your answer.

4. Use context to determine the meaning of the word **groveling** as it is used in *A Raisin in the Sun*. Write your definition of *groveling* here and explain how you arrived at it.

5. Use context to determine the meaning of the word **epitaph** as it is used in *A Raisin in the Sun*. Double check your answer using a dictionary. In your own words, write a definition of *epitaph* here.

Please note that excerpts and passages in the StudySync® library and this workbook are intended as touchstones to generate interest in an author's work. The excerpts and passages do not substitute for the reading of entire texts, and StudySync® strongly recommends that students seek out and purchase the whole literary or informational work in order to experience it as the author intended. Links to online resellers are available in our digital library. In addition, complete works may be ordered through an authorized reseller by filling out and returning to StudySync® the order form enclosed in this workbook.

Reading & Writing Companion 61

Skill: Dramatic Elements and Structure

Use the Checklist to analyze Dramatic Elements and Structure in *A Raisin in the Sun*. Refer to the sample student annotations about Dramatic Elements and Structure in the text.

••• CHECKLIST FOR DRAMATIC ELEMENTS AND STRUCTURE

In order to determine the author's choices regarding the development of a drama, note the following:

- ✓ the names of all the characters, how they are introduced, and their relationships with one another

- ✓ character development, including personality traits, motivations, decisions they make, and actions they take

- ✓ the setting(s) of the story and how it influences the characters and the events of the plot

- ✓ how characters' choices and dialogue affect the plot

- ✓ the stage directions and how they are used to reveal character and plot development

To analyze the impact of the author's choices regarding how to develop and relate elements of a story or drama, consider the following questions:

- ✓ How does the order of events in the play affect the development of the drama?

- ✓ How are characters introduced, and what does it reveal about them?

- ✓ In what ways do the characters change over the course of the drama?

- ✓ How do the choices the characters make help advance the plot?

- ✓ How does the setting affect the characters and plot?

- ✓ How do the characters' actions help develop the theme or message of the play?

Skill: Dramatic Elements and Structure

Reread paragraph 17 of *A Raisin in the Sun*. Then, using the Checklist on the previous page, answer the multiple-choice questions below.

⟳ YOUR TURN

1. Which of the following sentences best describes the relationship between the dialogue and the stage directions in this passage?

   ○ A. The dialogue and the stage directions complement each other to reinforce that Walter feels confident about his accepting the money from Mr. Lindner.

   ○ B. The aggressive mockery in the dialogue and the anguished horror of the stage directions reflect the extreme pain of Walter's conflict.

   ○ C. The dialogue and the stage directions work together to show that Ruth, Bennie, and Mama agree with Walter.

   ○ D. The painful dialogue and emotional stage directions show that the family is falling apart.

2. The relationship between the dialogue and the stage directions in this passage advances the plot by—

   ○ A. bringing the plot in this scene to its climax, or the point at which the conflict reaches its highest tension.

   ○ B. providing a resolution to the conflict.

   ○ C. giving background information, or exposition, about Walter's emotional state.

   ○ D. wrapping up loose ends in the falling action.

Please note that excerpts and passages in the StudySync® library and this workbook are intended as touchstones to generate interest in an author's work. The excerpts and passages do not substitute for the reading of entire texts, and StudySync® strongly recommends that students seek out and purchase the whole literary or informational work in order to experience it as the author intended. Links to online resellers are available in our digital library. In addition, complete works may be ordered through an authorized reseller by filling out and returning to StudySync® the order form enclosed in this workbook.

Reading & Writing Companion   **63**

Skill:
Theme

Use the Checklist to analyze Theme in *A Raisin in the Sun*. Refer to the sample student annotation about Theme in the text.

Copyright © BookheadEd Learning, LLC

••• CHECKLIST FOR THEME

In order to identify two or more themes, or central ideas, of a text, note the following:

✓ the subject and how it relates to the themes in the text

✓ if one or more themes is stated directly in the text

✓ details in the text that help reveal each theme:

- the title and chapter headings

- details about the setting

- the narrator's or speaker's tone

- characters' thoughts, actions, and dialogue

- the central conflict, climax, and resolution of the conflict

- shifts in characters, setting, or plot events

✓ when the themes interact with each other

To determine two or more themes, or central ideas, of a text and to analyze their development over the course of the text, including how they interact and build on one another to produce a complex account, consider the following questions:

✓ What are the themes in the text? When do they emerge?

✓ How does each theme develop over the course of the text?

✓ How do the themes interact and build on one another?

Skill: Theme

Reread paragraphs 9–15 of *A Raisin in the Sun*. Then, using the Checklist on the previous page, answer the multiple-choice questions below.

⟳ YOUR TURN

1. Which inference best demonstrates the relationship between characters and the theme about manhood as seen in paragraph 11?

   ○ A. Walter does not think sharecroppers are considered men.
   ○ B. Walter wants to win over his wife's affection by buying her pearls.
   ○ C. Walter acknowledges that all men want to own a yacht.
   ○ D. Walter prioritizes the expectation of proving his manhood by providing for his wife.

2. Beneatha's comments in paragraph 10 reveal that—

   ○ A. the characters live in a racially segregated neighborhood.
   ○ B. someone died in the house.
   ○ C. their home used to have a hopeful atmosphere.
   ○ D. there is no natural lighting in the house.

3. Which paragraph best communicates the message that being poor doesn't necessitate a loss of dignity and self-respect?

   ○ A. 9
   ○ B. 12
   ○ C. 13
   ○ D. 14

Close Read

Reread *A Raisin in the Sun*. As you reread, complete the Skills Focus questions below. Then use your answers and annotations from the questions to help you complete the Write activity.

◎ SKILLS FOCUS

1. Highlight an exchange of dialogue between Beneatha and Walter that shows how Beneatha feels about the family's dreams and Walter's reaction. Analyze the relationship between plot and theme in these lines.

2. Identify a passage that includes dialogue and stage directions that show what Walter thinks it means to be a man. Analyze how these dramatic elements help advance the plot of the play.

3. Locate a passage that contains clues about the setting of *A Raisin in the Sun*. How does the setting affect the characters and influence the plot?

4. Identify dialogue between Beneatha and Mama near the end of the scene in which they discuss respect, dignity, and love. Analyze the relationship between characters, and explain how their exchange reveals a theme of the play.

5. Why is owning a home so important to Mama? What makes a home so important to a family? Identify textual evidence to support your answer.

✏ WRITE

LITERARY ANALYSIS: In both *Death of a Salesman* and *A Raisin in the Sun*, dialogue plays an important role in the development of the texts' themes. Analyze how dialogue reflects each text's message about the importance of family and the relevance of the American Dream. Support your response with the most relevant evidence from the text and your own analysis.

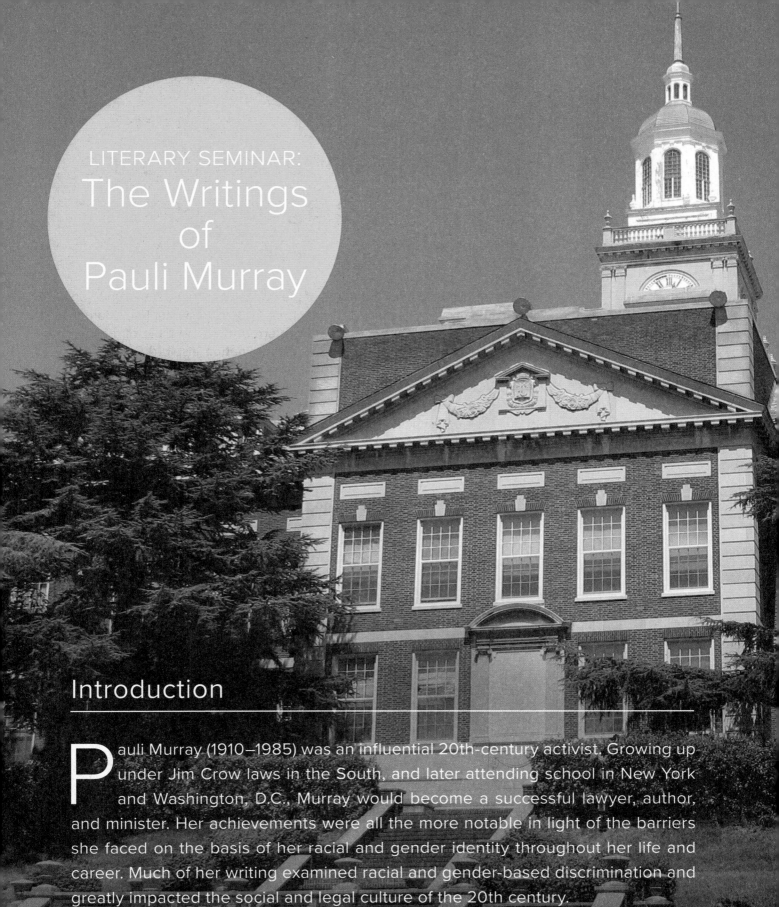

LITERARY SEMINAR:
The Writings of Pauli Murray

Introduction

Pauli Murray (1910–1985) was an influential 20th-century activist. Growing up under Jim Crow laws in the South, and later attending school in New York and Washington, D.C., Murray would become a successful lawyer, author, and minister. Her achievements were all the more notable in light of the barriers she faced on the basis of her racial and gender identity throughout her life and career. Much of her writing examined racial and gender-based discrimination and greatly impacted the social and legal culture of the 20th century.

"Now, how do I go about killing 'Jane Crow'—prejudice against sex."

1   One of the most influential members of the civil rights movement is a person whose name might not be familiar: the activist, lawyer, and writer Pauli Murray. She wrote the book Thurgood Marshall referred to as the bible of the civil rights movement and her work on sex **discrimination** inspired Ruth Bader Ginsburg to cite her in the first legal brief Ginsburg argued before the Supreme Court. She was friends with Eleanor Roosevelt and Langston Hughes, served on a Presidential Commission appointed by John F. Kennedy, and she helped launch the National Organization for Women with Betty Friedan, as well as the Congress for Racial Equality. Murray's impact can be traced through a dynamic body of writing increasingly available to readers today.

Pauli Murray, c. 1940s

Early Advocacy

2   Pauli Murray's desire to fight against racial and sex discrimination began early, as she encountered barrier after barrier that restricted her personal, educational, and career opportunities. As a young woman, she hoped to escape the segregation of Jim Crow laws in the South and attend Columbia in New York City, but discovered that the school did not admit women and

attended Hunter College instead. Graduating at the height of the Great Depression, she struggled to find work, and decided to return home and apply for a graduate program in sociology at the University of North Carolina–Chapel Hill.

3 However, Murray was denied her admission to the graduate school because of her race. She leveraged writing as a tool to challenge the decision, waging a letter-writing campaign in 1938 protesting UNC's decision. Coincidentally, two days prior to UNC's rejection of Murray, the Supreme Court had ruled that colleges must either admit or supply equivalent education to non-white students. Murray published letters she sent and received to the school's officials and to prominent public figures, such as President Roosevelt, bringing national attention to the issue. Eventually, UNC avoided having to admit Murray or other African American students when it made **provisions** for what it deemed an equivalent program in Durham, North Carolina, and so satisfied the court's ruling. While she was frustrated by the outcome, Murray's efforts earned the attention of Eleanor Roosevelt, with whom she eventually became friends. Murray advised on matters of civil and human rights until Roosevelt's passing.

4 Although her writing brought attention to her ideas and intellect, one particular aspect of her identity often kept her from the activist spotlight. Murray often expressed her gender identity as male, though she frequently saw her experiences through the female lens. On a bus trip in 1940 to visit her aunt in Virginia, Murray and a female companion were arrested for refusing to move to the back of the bus. At the time, Murray was passing as male and gave her name as Oliver Fleming to the arresting officer. Murray and her companion were jailed for three days, and during their time in jail, used the principles of *satyagraha* (passive political resistance) to write three letters: one to their jailers, one to their fellow prisoners, and another detailing the facts of the case as Murray saw them. Although lawyers from the NAACP remarked her notes were "as good as a lawyer's brief," the NAACP ultimately elected to not support an appeal. Murray suspected that the NAACP's hesitance to become involved was due to fears they would need to discuss her gender performance as a man. The writing she generated throughout the experience, however, demonstrates the developing nonviolent resistance strategies she **espoused**.

The Challenges of Jane Crow

5 Through Murray's passion for social justice and eloquent speaking, she gained respect from important figures of the day and learned the nuances of the legal issues behind segregation. She worked for the Workers Defense League, a non-profit labor organization that campaigned to commute the death sentence of Odell Waller, who had been convicted of first-degree murder in a one-day trial by an all-white jury. She toured the South, speaking

Please note that excerpts and passages in the StudySync® library and this workbook are intended as touchstones to generate interest in an author's work. The excerpts and passages do not substitute for the reading of entire texts, and StudySync® strongly recommends that students seek out and purchase the whole literary or informational work in order to experience it as the author intended. Links to online resellers are available in our digital library. In addition, complete works may be ordered through an authorized reseller by filling out and returning to StudySync® the order form enclosed in this workbook.

Reading & Writing Companion

69

publicly and meeting with lawyers, including Dr. Leon Ransom, the dean of Howard University School of Law. Dr. Ransom was so impressed with her arguments that he promised her a fellowship to study law at Howard.

6   It was at Howard that Murray gained the personal experience that helped build her influential legal arguments against sex discrimination. While Murray was no longer in the racial minority at Howard University Law, she was the only female student, and was blocked from opportunities despite her high achievement, a phenomenon she began to refer to as "Jane Crow." Upon graduating top of her class, she was denied from post-graduate studies at Harvard Law School due to her sex, and engaged in another campaign like the one against UNC to challenge this discrimination. Even with a letter of support from President Franklin Roosevelt, however, she lost her appeal.

7   While in law school, Murray wrote a paper for Dr. Ransom, arguing that segregation violated the Thirteenth and Fourteenth Amendments of the United States Constitution because "separate" was inherently not "equal." Murray's argument shifted the focus away from the equality of various segregated institutions, a legal strategy that the NAACP had been working to combat segregationist policies for years. As she submitted this paper to Dr. Ransom, Murray included a short note that revealed her beliefs about the relationship between race and sex and predicted a major legacy of her work, asking, "Now, how do I go about killing 'Jane Crow'—prejudice against sex."

Writing Change

8   After being denied from Harvard and completing a Master's of Law at University of California—Berkeley, Murray wrote one of her most consequential texts. The Women's Division of the Methodist Church asked Murray to research the laws of segregation, with the expectation being a simple pamphlet. Murray went above and beyond, writing the *States' Laws on Race and Color*, a several hundred page examination of all state laws that involved race. Murray went against the grain of historical precedent that relied almost exclusively on legal arguments, and used psychological and sociological evidence to argue that race was an **arbitrary** classification, and therefore racial segregation was unconstitutional.

9   Thurgood Marshall, who would later become the first African American justice on the Supreme Court, called the book the bible of civil rights, lawyers keeping stacks of it around the NAACP offices as his team argued *Brown v. Board of Education*. A member of Marshall's legal team and a former professor of Murray's at Howard, Spottswood Robinson remembered Murray's paper for Dr. Ransom on the Thirteenth and Fourteenth Amendments and shared it with his colleagues. The lawyers on the case were inspired by Murray's

arguments, and the Supreme Court overturned *Plessy v. Ferguson*, the case from which "separate but equal" had come.

10 Murray continued to use legal arguments to fight race and sex discrimination. Some in the civil rights movement believed that including sex as a protected class would prevent the Civil Rights Act of 1964 from passing, but Murray wrote a widely circulated memo arguing that without the inclusion of sex as a protected class, black women would not be protected under the bill. Murray's memo helped convince **skeptics** in the White House and Congress that the provision regarding sex was not just an add-on, and in fact, was necessary to achieving the bill's goals. The bill passed, banning segregation in public places and employment discrimination, including sex discrimination.

(Back, left to right) Professor Albert M. Sacks, Pauli Murray, Dr. Mary Bunting; (seated) Alma Lutz, Betty Friedan. Harvard Law School Forum speaking event

11 Murray's writing would further influence policy. While finishing her doctorate in law at Yale University, Murray co-wrote "Jane Crow and the Law: Sex Discrimination and Title VII," which helped create a legal basis for ending sex discrimination. Murray would go on to serve as co-counsel on a highly influential case, *White v. Crook*, with Dorothy Kenyon in 1965 that would successfully eliminate the use of sex and race discrimination in jury selection. Eventually, this work would get recognition, with Ruth Bader Ginsburg naming Pauli Murray and Dorothy Kenyon as co-authors on the *Reed v. Reed* brief to the Supreme Court in 1971, acknowledging their contributions to the fight against sex discrimination.

Considering Murray's Legacy

12   The question must be asked: Why isn't Pauli Murray a more well-known figure? Recently, Murray's contributions to, and her personal involvement in, the civil rights movement have been more widely recognized. For example, the 2018 movie dramatizing Ruth Bader Ginsburg's first gender-discrimination argument in court, *On the Basis of Sex*, depicted Murray, played by Sharon Washington, advising on Ginsburg's strategy in court. One possible reason that much of Murray's work was behind-the-scenes is that contemporary attitudes about her identity as a queer[1] African American woman kept her from the spotlight.

13   Fortunately for today's readers, Murray generated a great deal of writing, including over 300 letters with Eleanor Roosevelt, two autobiographies, and a book of poetry. The publication of these works has led to renewed interest in her work. Murray's writings provide insight into a multifaceted leader, who had a hand in many social and legal advances during the twentieth century.

Copyright © BookheadEd Learning, LLC

---

1 Murray's memoirs and history suggest that today she most likely would have identified as "queer" or "transgender." Here, the term "queer" is used in the modern sense as an all-encompassing term for individuals who do not identify as heterosexual or are gender non-conforming.

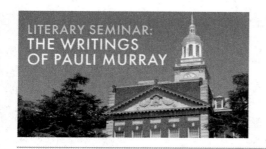

Literary Seminar: The Writings of Pauli Murray

Read "Literary Seminar: The Writings of Pauli Murray." After you read, complete the Think Questions below.

☁ THINK QUESTIONS

1. Who is Dr. Leon Ransom, and how did he help Pauli Murray along her journey to achieve social and legal advancements? Support your answer with evidence from the text.

2. What is *satyagraha*, and how was it successful in Pauli Murray's case? Cite evidence from the text to support your answer.

3. What is Pauli Murray's most consequential achievement, and how did it come about? Explain using relevant evidence from the text.

4. What is the meaning of the word **arbitrary** as it is used in the text? Write your best definition here, along with a brief explanation of how you arrived at its meaning.

5. Read the following dictionary entry:

provision
pro•vi•sion /pruh-vizh-uhn/

noun

1. the ability to produce something useful
2. a quantity that is furnished or supplied

verb

1. to present with sustenance, namely meals, liquids, or supplies, particularly for a trip
2. to put something out of the way, especially a quantity that is specifically designated to cover an organization's finances of a known debt or liability

Which definition most closely matches **provision** as it is used in the text? Write that definition of *provision* here and indicate which clues found in the text helped you determine its meaning.

Please note that excerpts and passages in the StudySync® library and this workbook are intended as touchstones to generate interest in an author's work. The excerpts and passages do not substitute for the reading of entire texts, and StudySync® strongly recommends that students seek out and purchase the whole literary or informational work in order to experience it as the author intended. Links to online resellers are available in our digital library. In addition, complete works may be ordered through an authorized reseller by filling out and returning to StudySync® the order form enclosed in this workbook.

Reading & Writing Companion   73

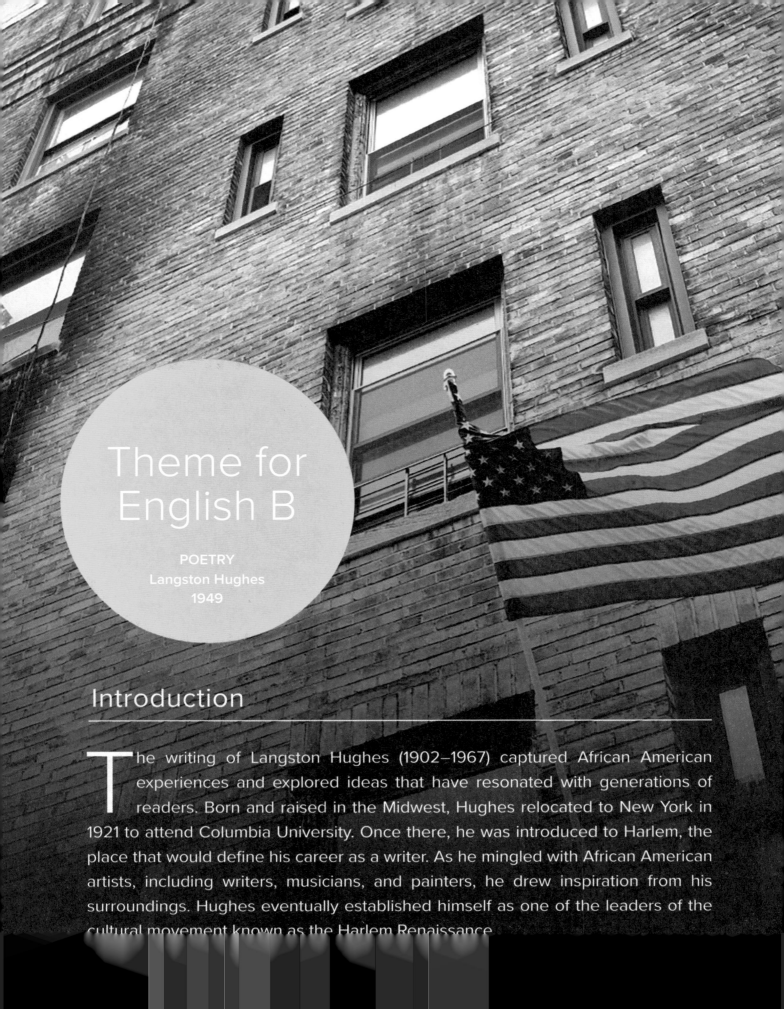

Theme for English B

POETRY
Langston Hughes
1949

Introduction

The writing of Langston Hughes (1902–1967) captured African American experiences and explored ideas that have resonated with generations of readers. Born and raised in the Midwest, Hughes relocated to New York in 1921 to attend Columbia University. Once there, he was introduced to Harlem, the place that would define his career as a writer. As he mingled with African American artists, including writers, musicians, and painters, he drew inspiration from his surroundings. Hughes eventually established himself as one of the leaders of the cultural movement known as the Harlem Renaissance.

"Sometimes perhaps you don't want to be a part of me. / Nor do I often want to be a part of you."

NOTES

1 The instructor said,
2 Go home and write
3 a page tonight.
4 And let that page come out of you—
5 Then, it will be true.

6 I wonder if it's that **simple**?
7 I am twenty-two, **colored**[1], born in Winston-Salem.
8 I went to school there, then Durham, then here
9 to this college on the hill above Harlem.
10 I am the only colored student in my class.
11 The steps from the hill lead down into Harlem,
12 through a park, then I cross St. Nicholas,
13 Eighth Avenue, Seventh, and I come to the Y,
14 the Harlem Branch Y, where I take the elevator
15 up to my room, sit down, and write this page:

16 It's not easy to know what is true for you or me
17 at twenty-two, my age. But I guess I'm what
18 I feel and see and hear, Harlem, I hear you:
19 hear you, hear me—we two—you, me, talk on this page.
20 (I hear New York, too.) Me—who?
21 Well, I like to eat, sleep, drink, and be in love.
22 I like to work, read, learn, and understand life.
23 I like a pipe for a Christmas present,
24 or records—Bessie[2], bop, or Bach.
25 I guess being colored doesn't make me not like
26 the same things other folks like who are other races.
27 So will my page be colored that I write?

---

1. **colored** a term that was common at the time, used to describe someone who was racially non-white, usually black
2. **Bessie** Bessie Smith, a well-known jazz and blues singer from the 1920s and 1930s

NOTES

28 Being me, it will not be white.

29 But it will be

30 a part of you, instructor.

31 You are white—

32 yet a part of me, as I am a part of you.

33 That's American.

34 Sometimes perhaps you don't want to be a part of me.

35 Nor do I often want to be a part of you.

36 But we are, that's true!

37 As I learn from you,

38 I guess you learn from me—

39 although you're older—and white—

40 and somewhat more free.

41 This is my page for English B.

"Theme for English B" from THE COLLECTED POEMS OF LANGSTON HUGHES by Langston Hughes, edited by Arnold Rampersad with David Roessel, Associate Editor, copyright © 1994 by the Estate of Langston Hughes. Used by permission of Alfred A. Knopf, an imprint of the Knopf Doubleday Publishing Group, a division of Random House LLC. All rights reserved.

By permission of Harold Ober Associates Incorporated.
Copyright © 1994 by The Estate of Langston Hughes.

✏ WRITE

PERSONAL RESPONSE: Throughout his poem "Theme for English B," Langston Hughes addresses the complicated dynamics of the speaker's experience as the only student of color in his college class. Write a personal response in which you reflect on your own experience with a contemporary social issue. Include descriptive details and figurative language to create a rich and meaningful response.

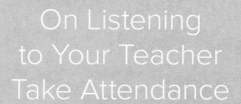

On Listening to Your Teacher Take Attendance

POETRY
Aimee Nezhukumatathil
2018

Introduction

Aimee Nezhukumatathil (b. 1974) was born in Chicago to a Filipina mother and an Indian father. She is the author of three collections of poetry and currently serves as a professor in the MFA program at the University of Mississippi. In this poem, Nezhukumatathil uses vivid imagery and detail to evoke the speaker's feelings as her last name is mispronounced by yet another teacher.

"... And when / everyone turns around to check out / your face, no need to flush red and warm."

1 Breathe deep even if it means you wrinkle
2 your nose from the fake-lemon **antiseptic**

3 of the mopped floors and wiped-down
4 doorknobs. The freshly soaped necks

5 and armpits. Your teacher means well,
6 even if he **butchers** your name like

7 he has a bloody sausage casing stuck
8 between his teeth, handprints

9 on his white, sloppy apron. And when
10 everyone turns around to check out

11 your face, no need to flush red and warm.
12 Just picture all the eyes as if your classroom

13 is one big scallop with its dozens of icy blues
14 and you will remember that winter your family

15 took you to the China Sea and you sank
16 your face in it to gaze at baby clams and sea stars

17 the size of your **outstretched** hand. And when
18 all those necks start to **crane**, try not to forget

19 someone once **lathered** their bodies, once patted them
20 dry with a fluffy towel after a bath, set out their clothes

21 for the first day of school. Think of their pencil cases
22 from third grade, full of sharp pencils, a pink pearl eraser.

23 Think of their handheld pencil sharpener and its tiny blade.

✏️ WRITE

POETRY: Sometimes writing in the second person makes describing painful situations easier because it takes the focus off the speaker. The second person can also be used to give comfort, advice, or instruction to others. Using "On Listening to Your Teacher Take Attendance" as a guide, write a poem in the second person about a real or imagined situation in which the narrator describes personal memories, thoughts, or actions. Be sure to maintain the second-person voice and use descriptive language throughout your poem.

Please note that excerpts and passages in the StudySync® library and this workbook are intended as touchstones to generate interest in an author's work. The excerpts and passages do not substitute for the reading of entire texts, and StudySync® strongly recommends that students seek out and purchase the whole literary or informational work in order to experience it as the author intended. Links to online resellers are available in our digital library. In addition, complete works may be ordered through an authorized reseller by filling out and returning to StudySync® the order form enclosed in this workbook.

Reading & Writing Companion   **79**

Brown v. Board of Education

ARGUMENTATIVE TEXT
U.S. Supreme Court
1954

Introduction

A class-action suit filed by 13 Topeka, Kansas, parents on behalf of their children, *Brown v. Board of Education* was a landmark 1954 U.S. Supreme Court case that declared unanimously, with no dissenting opinions, that establishing separate public schools for African American students was unconstitutional. The ruling overturned the previous *Plessy v. Ferguson* decision from 1896, which sanctioned segregation in public institutions.

"A sense of inferiority affects the motivation of a child to learn."

from the unanimous decision of the Court, delivered by Chief Justice Earl Warren:

1. In approaching this problem, we cannot turn the clock back to 1868, when the [Fourteenth] Amendment was adopted, or even to 1896, when *Plessy v. Ferguson* was written. We must consider public education in the light of its full development and its present place in American life throughout the Nation. Only in this way can it be determined if segregation in public schools deprives these plaintiffs of the equal protection of the laws.

Elizabeth Eckford ignores the hostile screams and stares of fellow students on her first day of school at Little Rock's Central High School.

2. Today, education is perhaps the most important function of state and local governments. Compulsory school attendance laws and the great expenditures for education both demonstrate our recognition of the importance of education to our democratic society. It is required in the performance of our most basic public responsibilities, even service in the armed forces. It is the very **foundation** of good citizenship. Today it is a principal instrument in awakening the child to cultural values, in preparing him for later professional training, and in helping him to adjust normally to his environment. In these days, it is doubtful that any child may reasonably be expected to succeed in life if he is denied the opportunity of an education. Such an opportunity, where the state has undertaken to provide it, is a right which must be made available to all on equal terms.

3. We come then to the question presented: Does segregation of children in public schools solely on the basis of race, even though the physical facilities and other **"tangible"** factors may be equal, deprive the children of the minority group of equal educational opportunities? We believe that it does.

Skill: Technical Language

The author mentions segregation in schools. Segregation shares a root with segregate, so it likely has to do with separating. The author does not mention who was separated or by what criteria.

Skill: Word Meaning

What does facilities mean here? I know the term is used as a noun in this sentence. The facilities are described as physical and have to do with public schools. Maybe the word refers to the school building.

Reading & Writing Companion

Skill:
Reasons and
Evidence

The claim is
strengthened by citing
previous court cases.
Both cases point out
that there are negative
effects of segregation,
which are hard to
measure. This supports
the claim that
segregation is
inherently unequal.

4   In *Sweatt v. Painter,* in finding that a segregated law school for Negroes could not provide them equal educational opportunities, this Court relied in large part on "those qualities which are incapable of objective measurement but which make for greatness in a law school." In *McLaurin v. Oklahoma State Regents,* the Court, in requiring that a Negro admitted to a white graduate school be treated like all other students, again resorted to intangible considerations: ". . . his ability to study, to engage in discussions and exchange views with other students, and, in general, to learn his profession." Such considerations apply with added force to children in grade and high schools. To separate them from others of similar age and qualifications solely because of their race generates a feeling of inferiority as to their status in the community that may affect their hearts and minds in a way unlikely ever to be undone. The effect of this separation on their educational opportunities was well stated by a finding in the Kansas case by a court which nevertheless felt compelled to rule against the Negro plaintiffs: Segregation of white and colored children in public schools has a **detrimental** effect upon the colored children. The impact is greater when it has the **sanction** of the law, for the policy of separating the races is usually interpreted as denoting the inferiority of the negro group. A sense of inferiority affects the motivation of a child to learn. Segregation with the sanction of law, therefore, has a tendency to [retard] the educational and mental development of negro children and to deprive them of some of the benefits they would receive in a racial[ly] integrated school system. Whatever may have been the extent of psychological knowledge at the time of *Plessy v. Ferguson,* this finding is amply supported by modern authority. Any language in *Plessy v. Ferguson* contrary to this finding is rejected.

5   We conclude that, in the field of public education, the doctrine of "separate but equal" has no place. Separate educational facilities are **inherently** unequal. Therefore, we hold that the plaintiffs and others similarly situated for whom the actions have been brought are, by reason of the segregation complained of, deprived of the equal protection of the laws guaranteed by the Fourteenth Amendment.

First Read

Read *Brown v. Board of Education*. After you read, complete the Think Questions below.

 THINK QUESTIONS

1. Why might the Supreme Court have thought that this ruling, overturning *Plessy v. Ferguson,* was important for the country? Refer to one or more details from the text to support your explanation.

2. According to Chief Justice Warren, what effect did a court ruling such as *Plessy v. Ferguson* have on educational opportunities for students? Support your answer with textual evidence.

3. Use details and evidence provided in the text to explain what Chief Justice Warren means by the phrase "modern authority" at the end of the next-to-last paragraph.

4. What is the meaning of the word **tangible** as it is used in the text? Write your best definition here, along with a brief explanation of how you arrived at its meaning.

5. What is the meaning of the word **detrimental** as it is used in the text? Write your best definition here, along with a brief explanation of how you arrived at its meaning.

Skill:
Reasons and Evidence

Use the Checklist to analyze Reasons and Evidence in *Brown v. Board of Education*. Refer to the sample student annotations about Reasons and Evidence in the text.

••• CHECKLIST FOR REASONS AND EVIDENCE

In order to delineate and evaluate the reasoning and evidence in seminal U.S. texts, note the following:

✓ the writer's position and how he or she uses legal reasoning to interpret the law

- legal reasoning includes the thinking processes and strategies used by lawyers and judges when arguing and deciding legal cases and is based on constitutional principles, or laws written down in the U.S. Constitution

✓ whether the premise is based on legal reasoning and constitutional principles

✓ the precision of the author's argument or how exactly he or she identifies conflicts, claims, objections, and supporting evidence

✓ how compelling the writer's argument is, including the elements that give the argument force and power and those that lessen its strength and viability

To evaluate the reasoning and evidence in seminal U.S. texts, including the application of constitutional principles and use of legal reasoning, consider the following questions:

✓ What position does the writer take?

✓ How does the writer use constitutional principles and legal reasoning to support his or her position?

✓ What evidence does the author use to support his or her claim?

Skill:
Reasons and Evidence

Reread paragraphs 4 and 5 of *Brown v. Board of Education*. Then, using the Checklist on the previous page, answer the multiple-choice questions below.

⟳ YOUR TURN

1. What is the main claim made in the closing of this decision?

   ○ A. That the doctrine of "separate but equal" is unconstitutional as stipulated by the Fourteenth Amendment.

   ○ B. That the doctrine of "separate but equal" is constitutional as stipulated by the Fourteenth Amendment.

   ○ C. That the doctrine of "separate but equal" has no place in public education and is inherently racist.

   ○ D. That the doctrine of "separate but equal" has deprived the plaintiffs of a high-quality education.

2. Which line from the passage best represents the reasoning that Chief Justice Warren uses to support the claim of this unanimous decision?

   ○ A. "Segregation of white and colored children in public schools has a detrimental effect upon the colored children."

   ○ B. "The impact is greater when it has the sanction of the law, for the policy of separating the races is usually interpreted as denoting the inferiority of the negro group."

   ○ C. "A sense of inferiority affects the motivation of a child to learn."

   ○ D. "Whatever may have been the extent of psychological knowledge at the time of *Plessy v. Ferguson,* this finding is amply supported by modern authority."

Please note that excerpts and passages in the StudySync® library and this workbook are intended as touchstones to generate interest in an author's work. The excerpts and passages do not substitute for the reading of entire texts, and StudySync® strongly recommends that students seek out and purchase the whole literary or informational work in order to experience it as the author intended. Links to online resellers are available in our digital library. In addition, complete works may be ordered through an authorized reseller by filling out and returning to StudySync® the order form enclosed in this workbook.

Skill:
Technical Language

Use the Checklist to analyze Technical Language in *Brown v. Board of Education*. Refer to the sample student annotations about Technical Language in the text.

••• CHECKLIST FOR TECHNICAL LANGUAGE

In order to determine the meanings of words and phrases as they are used in a text, including technical meanings, note the following:

- ✓ the subject of the text

- ✓ any unfamiliar words that you think might be technical terms

- ✓ words that have multiple meanings that change when used with a specific subject

- ✓ the possible contextual meaning of a word, or the definition from a dictionary

To determine the meanings of words and phrases as they are used in a text, including technical meanings, consider the following questions:

- ✓ What is the subject of the informational text?

- ✓ How does the use of technical language help establish the author as an authority on a subject?

- ✓ Are there any technical words that have an impact on the meaning and tone of the text?

- ✓ Does the author use the same term several times, refining its meaning and adding layers to it over the course of the text?

Skill:
Technical Language

Reread this passage from paragraph 4 of *Brown v. Board of Education*. Then, using the Checklist on the previous page, answer the multiple-choice questions below.

↻ YOUR TURN

from *Brown v. Board of Education* by U.S. Supreme Court

. . . The impact is greater when it has the sanction of the law, for the policy of separating the races is usually interpreted as denoting the inferiority of the negro group. A sense of inferiority affects the motivation of a child to learn. Segregation with the sanction of law, therefore, has a tendency to [retard] the educational and mental development of negro children and to deprive them of some of the benefits they would receive in a racial[ly] integrated school system. Whatever may have been the extent of psychological knowledge at the time of *Plessy v. Ferguson,* this finding is amply supported by modern authority. Any language in *Plessy v. Ferguson* contrary to this finding is rejected.

1. How does the author further refine the meaning of the word *segregation* as it is used in this passage?

   ○ A. The author refines the meaning of the word *segregation* by mentioning it several times, illustrating the importance of the word in the text.

   ○ B. The phrase "segregation with the sanction of law" confirms that as it is used here, the word does not describe mere discrimination but institutionalized racism.

   ○ C. The author refines the meaning of the word *segregation* by defining it for the audience.

   ○ D. The phrase "separating the races" serves to clarify by what means people are being segregated.

2. Using context clues, determine the meaning of *integrated* as it is used in this passage.

   ○ A. with various parts or aspects linked or coordinated

   ○ B. desegregated

   ○ C. indicating the mean value or total sum of a measurement

   ○ D. two things combined so that they become a whole

Please note that excerpts and passages in the StudySync® library and this workbook are intended as touchstones to generate interest in an author's work. The excerpts and passages do not substitute for the reading of entire texts, and StudySync® strongly recommends that students seek out and purchase the whole literary or informational work in order to experience it as the author intended. Links to online resellers are available in our digital library. In addition, complete works may be ordered through an authorized reseller by filling out and returning to StudySync® the order form enclosed in this workbook.

Reading & Writing
Companion

87

Skill:
Word Meaning

Use the Checklist to analyze Word Meaning in *Brown v. Board of Education*. Refer to the sample student annotations about Word Meaning in the text.

••• CHECKLIST FOR WORD MEANING

In order to find the pronunciation of a word or to determine or clarify its precise meaning, do the following:

- ✓ determine the word's part of speech

- ✓ use context clues to make an inferred meaning of the word or phrase

- ✓ consult a dictionary to verify your preliminary determination of the meaning of a word or phrase

- ✓ be sure to read all of the definitions, and then decide which definition makes sense within the context of the text

In order to determine or to clarify a word's part of speech, do the following:

- ✓ determine what the word is describing

- ✓ identify how the word is being used in the phrase or sentence

In order to determine the etymology of a word, its origin, or its standard usage, do the following:

- ✓ use reference materials, such as a dictionary, to determine the word's origin and history

- ✓ consider how the historical context of the word clarifies its usage

To determine or to clarify the etymology or standard usage of a word, consider the following questions:

- ✓ How formal or informal is this word?

- ✓ What is the word describing? What inferred meanings can I make?

- ✓ In what context is the word being used?

- ✓ Is this slang? An example of vernacular? In what other contexts might this word be used?

- ✓ What is the etymology of this word?

Copyright © BookheadEd Learning, LLC

Skill:
Word Meaning

Reread paragraph 4 of *Brown v. Board of Education*. Then, using the Checklist on the previous page as well as the dictionary entry below, answer the multiple-choice questions.

⟳ YOUR TURN

intangible /in'tan jə b(ə)l/ *adjective*

1. difficult or impossible to define or understand; vague and abstract
2. unable to be touched or grasped; not having physical presence
3. unearthly, supernatural

1. This question has two parts. First, answer Part A. Then, answer Part B.

   Part A: Which definition best fits the way the word *intangible* is used in paragraph 4?
   ○ A. Definition 1
   ○ B. Definition 2
   ○ C. Definition 3
   ○ D. None of the above

   Part B: Which of the following phrases provides context that best explains the meaning of *intangible* as identified in Part A?
   ○ A. "could not provide them equal educational opportunities"
   ○ B. "incapable of objective measurement"
   ○ C. "a Negro admitted to a white graduate school"
   ○ D. "be treated like all other students"

Please note that excerpts and passages in the StudySync® library and this workbook are intended as touchstones to generate interest in an author's work. The excerpts and passages do not substitute for the reading of entire texts, and StudySync® strongly recommends that students seek out and purchase the whole literary or informational work in order to experience it as the author intended. Links to online resellers are available in our digital library. In addition, complete works may be ordered through an authorized reseller by filling out and returning to StudySync® the order form enclosed in this workbook.

Reading & Writing
Companion

89

Close Read

Reread *Brown v. Board of Education*. As you reread, complete the Skills Focus questions below. Then use your answers and annotations from the questions to help you complete the Write activity.

◎ SKILLS FOCUS

1. Infer the meaning of the word *plaintiffs* as it is used in the text. Explain why the use of this technical language is appropriate for this text.

2. Write a definition for the word *instrument* as it is used in paragraph 2. Highlight the clues in the text that helped you arrive at this definition. Then confirm your definition in a dictionary or online resource.

3. Identify an instance in the text where the author references another court case. How does the author use this piece of evidence to support his claim?

4. Identify one reason the author gives to support the idea that "separate" can never be "equal." Explain how the author's reasoning makes his argument more convincing.

5. Identify the goal(s) that the *Brown v. Board of Education* decision hoped to accomplish. Include information from the text to support your answer.

✏ WRITE

LITERARY ANALYSIS: After reading *Brown v. Board of Education*, "On Listening to Your Teacher Take Attendance," and "Theme for English B," write a brief essay in which you analyze the language of the court's decision. Make an argument about how it affects students' real-life experiences in school, using Nezhukumatathil's, Hughes's, and your own point of view to inform your argument. What was the intention conveyed by the ruling's language, and what does school look like in our country today? Demonstrate your understanding of the language of the ruling and support your argument using the most relevant evidence from the texts.

Civil Rights Act of 1964

INFORMATIONAL TEXT
Lyndon B. Johnson
with U.S. Congress
1964

Introduction

studysync TV

Easily the most memorable achievement of United States President Lyndon B. Johnson (1908–1973) was his role in the Civil Rights Act of 1964. Johnson famously signed the act into law, which banned discrimination based on race, national origin, religion, and gender in public places. The signing of this act also paved the way for Congress to pass the Voting Rights Act in 1965. Although the Civil Rights Act of 1964 was initially introduced during the presidency of Johnson's predecessor, John F. Kennedy, Johnson continued the fight against segregation in America in the wake of Kennedy's assassination. The following text includes the sections of the legislation that address the banning of discrimination in public places.

"All persons shall be entitled to be free, at any establishment or place, from discrimination . . ."

NOTES

1 **SEC. 201.** (a) All persons shall be entitled to the full and equal enjoyment of the goods, services, facilities, and privileges, advantages, and accommodations of any place of public accommodation, as defined in this section, without **discrimination** or segregation on the ground of race, color, religion, or national origin.

Clergy members stand in front as a crowd protesting for civil rights moves toward the Boston Common in Boston, April 23, 1965.

2 (b) Each of the following establishments which serves the public is a place of public accommodation within the meaning of this title if its operations affect commerce, or if discrimination or segregation by it is supported by State action:

3 (1) any inn, hotel, motel, or other establishment which provides lodging to **transient** guests, other than an establishment located within a building which contains not more than five rooms for rent or hire and which is actually occupied by the proprietor of such establishment as his residence;

4 (2) any restaurant, cafeteria, lunchroom, lunch counter, soda fountain, or other facility principally engaged in selling food for consumption on the premises, including, but not limited to, any such facility located on the premises of any retail establishment; or any gasoline station;

5 (3) any motion picture house[1], theater, concert hall, sports arena, stadium or other place of exhibition or entertainment; and

6 (4) any establishment (A)(i) which is physically located within the premises of any establishment otherwise covered by this subsection, or (ii) within the premises of which is physically located any such covered establishment, and (B) which holds itself out as serving patrons of such covered establishment.

---

1. **motion picture house** a single-screen movie theater

7   (c) The operations of an establishment affect commerce within the meaning of this title if (1) it is one of the establishments described in paragraph (1) of subsection (b); (2) in the case of an establishment described in paragraph (2) of subsection (b), it serves or offers to serve interstate travelers or a **substantial** portion of the food which it serves, or gasoline or other products which it sells, has moved in commerce; (3) in the case of an establishment described in paragraph (3) of subsection (b), it customarily presents films, performances, athletic teams, exhibitions, or other sources of entertainment which move in commerce; and (4) in the case of an establishment described in paragraph (4) of subsection (b), it is physically located within the premises of, or there is physically located within its premises, an establishment the operations of which affect commerce within the meaning of this subsection. For purposes of this section, "commerce" means travel, trade, traffic, commerce, transportation, or communication among the several States, or between the District of Columbia and any State, or between any foreign country or any territory or possession and any State or the District of Columbia, or between points in the same State but through any other State or the District of Columbia or a foreign country.

8   (d) Discrimination or segregation by an establishment is supported by State action within the meaning of this title if such discrimination or segregation (1) is carried on under color of any law[2], statute, ordinance, or regulation; or (2) is carried on under color of any custom or usage required or enforced by officials of the State or political subdivision thereof; or (3) is required by action of the State or political subdivision thereof.

9   (e) The provisions of this title shall not apply to a private club or other establishment not in fact open to the public, except to the extent that the facilities of such establishment are made available to the customers or patrons of an establishment within the **scope** of subsection (b).

10 **SEC. 202.** All persons shall be entitled to be free, at any establishment or place, from discrimination or segregation of any kind on the ground of race, color, religion, or national origin, if such discrimination or segregation is or purports to be required by any law, statute, ordinance, regulation, rule, or order of a State or any agency or political subdivision thereof.

11 **SEC. 203.** No person shall (a) withhold, deny, or attempt to withhold or deny, or deprive or attempt to deprive, any person of any right or privilege secured by section 201 or 202, or (b) intimidate, threaten, or coerce, or attempt to intimidate, threaten, or coerce any person with the purpose of interfering with

2. **under color of any law** with the appearance of legal power where it doesn't exist

Please note that excerpts and passages in the StudySync® library and this workbook are intended as touchstones to generate interest in an author's work. The excerpts and passages do not substitute for the reading of entire texts, and StudySync® strongly recommends that students seek out and purchase the whole literary or informational work in order to experience it as the author intended. Links to online resellers are available in our digital library. In addition, complete works may be ordered through an authorized reseller by filling out and returning to StudySync® the order form enclosed in this workbook.

Reading & Writing Companion   **93**

any right or privilege secured by section 201 or 202, or (c) punish or attempt to punish any person for exercising or attempting to exercise any right or privilege secured by section 201 or 202.

✎ WRITE

RESEARCH: The scope and specificity of the places named in this excerpt of the Civil Rights Act of 1964 serve not only to define the broad reach of the new law but also to recognize the particular battlegrounds where the fight for civil rights occurred. Research an event that took place in one of the locations mentioned in this portion of the Civil Rights Act of 1964. Then, write about how your research impacts your understanding of the text and the civil rights movement as a whole.

I've Been to the Mountaintop

ARGUMENTATIVE TEXT
Martin Luther King Jr.
1968

Introduction

Dr. Martin Luther King Jr. (1929–1968) delivered "I've Been to the Mountaintop" at Mason Temple in Memphis, Tennessee, on April 3, 1968. King had been to Memphis a number of times in the spring of 1968 to show his support for African American sanitation workers who were striking to protest unfair working conditions. On March 29, the situation in Memphis exploded when looters broke away from a protest march led by King and vandalized businesses on Beale Street. Chaos ensued, resulting in injuries, arrests, and the death of one man. Devastated by the violence, King returned to Memphis several days later to refocus the campaign on nonviolence and the plight of the sanitation workers. "I've Been to the Mountaintop" was King's last speech. He was assassinated on the evening of April 4, 1968, outside of his room at the Lorraine Motel in Memphis.

"We have an opportunity to make America a better nation."

NOTES

1   Thank you very kindly, my friends. As I listened to Ralph Abernathy[1] in his eloquent and generous introduction and then thought about myself, I wondered who he was talking about. It's always good to have your closest friend and associate to say something good about you. And Ralph Abernathy is the best friend that I have in the world.

2   I'm delighted to see each of you here tonight in spite of a storm warning. You reveal that you are determined to go on anyhow. Something is happening in Memphis; something is happening in our world.

3   And you know, if I were standing at the beginning of time, with the possibility of taking a kind of general and panoramic view of the whole of human history up to now, and the Almighty said to me, "Martin Luther King, which age would you like to live in?" I would take my mental flight by Egypt and I would watch God's children in their magnificent **trek** from the dark dungeons of Egypt through or rather across the Red Sea, through the wilderness on toward the promised land[2]. And in spite of its magnificence, I wouldn't stop there. I would move on by Greece and take my mind to Mount Olympus[3]. And I would see Plato, Aristotle, Socrates, Euripides and Aristophanes[4] assembled around the Parthenon, and I would watch them around the Parthenon[5], as they discussed the great and eternal issues of reality.

4   But I wouldn't stop there. I would go on, even to the great hey-day of the Roman Empire. And I would see **developments** around there, through various emperors and leaders. But I wouldn't stop there. I would even come up to the

1. **Ralph Abernathy** Civil rights leader Ralph Abernathy (1926–1990) was a mentor to Dr. King, and his successor as president of the Southern Christian Leadership Conference.
2. **"through the wilderness on toward the promised land"** a reference to the Book of Numbers in the Old Testament, in which the Israelites are made to wander in the wilderness for forty years before reaching their destination
3. **Mount Olympus** the highest mountain in Greece and the mythical residence of the Greek gods
4. **Plato, Aristotle, Socrates, Euripides and Aristophanes** great ancient Greek philosophers and playwrights, and the founders of Western thought
5. **Parthenon** 5th century B.C.E. temple on the Acropolis dedicated to the goddess Athena and dominating central Athens

day of the Renaissance, and get a quick picture of all that the Renaissance did for the cultural and esthetic life of man. But I wouldn't stop there. I would even go by the way that the man for whom I am named had his habitat. And I would watch Martin Luther as he tacked his ninety-five theses[6] on the door at the church of Wittenberg.

5 But I wouldn't stop there. I would come on up even to 1863, and watch a **vacillating** President by the name of Abraham Lincoln finally come to the conclusion that he had to sign the Emancipation Proclamation. But I wouldn't stop there. I would even come up to the early thirties, and see a man grappling with the problems of the bankruptcy of his nation. And come with an eloquent cry that we have nothing to fear but fear itself.

6 But I wouldn't stop there. Strangely enough, I would turn to the Almighty, and say, "If you allow me to live just a few years in the second half of the Twentieth Century, I will be happy." Now that's a strange statement to make, because the world is all messed up. The nation is sick. Trouble is in the land. Confusion all around. That's a strange statement. But I know, somehow, that only when it is dark enough can you see the stars. And I see God working in this period of the Twentieth Century in a way that men, in some strange way, are responding—something is happening in our world. The masses of people are rising up. And wherever they are assembled today, whether they are in Johannesburg, South Africa; Nairobi, Kenya; Accra, Ghana; New York City; Atlanta, Georgia; Jackson, Mississippi; or Memphis, Tennessee—the cry is always the same—"We want to be free."

7 Another reason that I'm happy to live in this period is that we have been forced to a point where we are going to have to grapple with the problems that men have been trying to grapple with through history, but the demands didn't force them to do it. Survival demands that we grapple with them. Men, for years now, have been talking about war and peace. But now, no longer can they just talk about it. It is no longer a choice between violence and nonviolence in this world, it's nonviolence or nonexistence.

8 That is where we are today. And also in the human rights revolution, if something isn't done, and done in a hurry, to bring the colored peoples of the world out of their long years of poverty, their long years of hurt and neglect, the whole world is doomed. Now, I'm just happy that God has allowed me to live in this period to see what is unfolding. And I'm happy that He's allowed me to be in Memphis.

Skill: Language, Style, and Audience

Grapple is used three times, and this repetition intensifies the call to action, as survival now depends on it. This engages the audience, and the serious tone suggests that choosing not to act peacefully could lead to nonexistence.

6. **ninety-five theses** proposals by theologian Martin Luther (1483–1546) that began the Protestant split from the Catholic Church

Skill: Central or Main Idea

King's main idea is introduced here. He is strongly stating that all people are God's children and should be treated equally. All human beings deserve to be treated decently, and he is determined to make this happen.

9   I can remember, I can remember when Negroes were just going around as Ralph has said so often, scratching where they didn't itch, and laughing when they were not tickled. But that day is all over. We mean business now, and we are determined to gain our rightful place in God's world.

10   And that's all this whole thing is about. We aren't engaged in any negative protest and in any negative arguments with anybody. We are saying that we are determined to be men. We are determined to be people. We are saying that we are God's children. And if we're God's children, we don't have to live like we are forced to live.

11   Now, what does all of this mean in this great period of history? It means that we've got to stay together. We've got to stay together and maintain unity. You know, whenever Pharaoh wanted to prolong the period of slavery in Egypt, he had a favorite, favorite formula for doing it. What was that? He kept the slaves fighting among themselves. But whenever the slaves get together, something happens in Pharaoh's court, and he cannot hold the slaves in slavery. When the slaves get together, that's the beginning of getting out of slavery. Now let us maintain unity.

12   Secondly, let us keep the issues where they are. The issue is injustice. The issue is the refusal of Memphis to be fair and honest in its dealings with its public servants, who happen to be sanitation workers. Now we've got to keep attention on that. That's always the problem with a little violence. You know what happened the other day, and the press dealt only with the window breaking. I read the articles. They very seldom got around to mentioning the fact that one thousand, three hundred sanitation workers are on strike, and that Memphis is not being fair to them, and that Mayor Loeb is in dire need of a doctor. They didn't get around to that.

13   Now we're going to march again, and we've got to march again, in order to put the issue where it is supposed to be. And force everybody to see that there are thirteen hundred of God's children here suffering, sometimes going hungry, going through dark and dreary nights wondering how this thing is going to come out. That's the issue. And we've got to say to the nation, "We know how it's coming out." For when people get caught up with that which is right and they are willing to sacrifice for it, there is no stopping point short of victory.

14   We aren't going to let any mace stop us. We are masters in our nonviolent movement in disarming police forces; they don't know what to do. I've seen them so often. I remember in Birmingham, Alabama, when we were in that majestic struggle there we would move out of the 16th Street Baptist Church

day after day, by the hundreds we would move out. And Bull Connor[7] would tell them to send the dogs forth, and they did come; but we just went before the dogs singing, "Ain't gonna let nobody turn me 'round." Bull Connor next would say, "Turn the fire hoses on." And as I said to you the other night, Bull Connor didn't know history. He knew a kind of physics that somehow didn't relate to the transphysics that we knew about. And that was the fact that there was a certain kind of fire that no water could put out. And we went before the fire hoses; we had known water. If we were Baptist or some other denominations, we had been immersed. If we were Methodist, and some others, we had been sprinkled, but we knew water.

15   That couldn't stop us. And we just went on before the dogs and we would look at them; and we'd go on before the water hoses and we would look at it, and we'd just go on singing "Over my head I see freedom in the air." And then we would be thrown in the paddy wagons, and sometimes we were stacked in there like sardines in a can. And they would throw us in, and old Bull would say, "Take them off," and they did; and we would just go in the paddy wagon singing, "We Shall Overcome." And every now and then we'd get in jail, and we'd see the jailers looking through the windows being moved by our prayers, and being moved by our words and our songs. And there was a power there which Bull Connor couldn't adjust to; and so we ended up transforming Bull into a steer, and we won our struggle in Birmingham.

16   Now we've got to go on in Memphis just like that. I call upon you to be with us when we go out Monday. Now about injunctions: We have an injunction and we're going into court tomorrow morning to fight this illegal, unconstitutional injunction. All we say to America is, "Be true to what you said on paper." If I lived in China or even Russia, or any totalitarian country, maybe I could understand some of these illegal injunctions. Maybe I could understand the denial of certain basic First Amendment privileges, because they hadn't committed themselves to that over there. But somewhere I read of the freedom of assembly. Somewhere I read of the freedom of speech. Somewhere I read of the freedom of press. Somewhere I read that the greatness of America is the right to protest for right. And so just as I say, we aren't going to let any dog or water hose turn us around, we aren't going to let any injunction turn us around. We are going on.

17   We need all of you. And you know what's beautiful to me, is to see all of these ministers of the Gospel. It's a marvelous picture. Who is it that is supposed to articulate the longings and aspirations of the people more than the preacher? Somehow the preacher must have a kind of fire shut up in his bones. And

Skill:
Rhetoric

King establishes credibility—uses ethos—by describing his persistence and victory in Birmingham, even in the face of extreme adversity. He uses ethos to persuade the audience to continue their nonviolent protests in Memphis.

---

7. **Bull Connor** Theophilus Eugene 'Bull' Connor (1897–1973) was Commissioner of Public Safety of Birmingham, Alabama, when he ordered the use of attack dogs and fire hoses against civil rights demonstrators in May of 1963.

whenever injustice is around he must tell it. Somehow the preacher must be an Amos, and say, "When God speaks who can but prophesy?" Again with Amos[8], "Let justice roll down like waters and righteousness like a mighty stream." Somehow the preacher must say with Jesus, "The Spirit of the Lord is upon me, because He hath anointed me to deal with the problems of the poor."

18 And I want to commend the preachers, under the leadership of these noble men: James Lawson, one who has been in this struggle for many years; he's been to jail for struggling; he's been kicked out of Vanderbilt University for this struggle, but he's still going on, fighting for the rights of his people. Reverend Ralph Jackson, Billy Kiles. I could just go right on down the list, but time will not permit. But I want to thank all of them. And I want you to thank them, because so often, preachers aren't concerned about anything but themselves. And I'm always happy to see a relevant ministry.

19 It's all right to talk about "long white robes over yonder,"[9] in all of its symbolism. But ultimately people want some suits and dresses and shoes to wear down here! It's all right to talk about "streets flowing with milk and honey,"[10] but God has commanded us to be concerned about the slums down here, and his children who can't eat three square meals a day. It's all right to talk about the New Jerusalem[11], but one day, God's preacher must talk about the new New York, the new Atlanta, the new Philadelphia, the new Los Angeles, the new Memphis, Tennessee. This is what we have to do.

20 Now the other thing we'll have to do is this. Always anchor our external direct action with the power of economic withdrawal. Now, we are poor people. Individually, we are poor when you compare us with white society in America. We are poor. Never stop and forget, that collectively, that means all of us together, collectively, we are richer than all the nations in the world, with the exception of nine. Did you ever think about that? After you leave the United States, Soviet Russia, Great Britain, West Germany, France, and I could name the others, the American Negro collectively is richer than most nations of the world. We have an annual income of more than thirty billion dollars a year, which is more than all of the exports of the United States, and more than the national budget of Canada. Did you know that? That's power right there, if we know how to pool it.

---

8. **Amos** one of the twelve prophets of the Old Testament
9. **"long white robes over yonder"** a reference to the belief in an afterlife in heaven as reward for earthly suffering
10. **"streets flowing with milk and honey"** In the Old Testament, God promised Abraham the land of Canaan (Israel) would "flow with milk and honey."
11. **New Jerusalem** In the Old Testament, Ezekiel says that there will one day be a New Jerusalem as capital of God's kingdom on Earth.

21 We don't have to argue with anybody. We don't have to curse and go around acting bad with our words. We don't need any bricks and bottles, we don't need any Molotov cocktails. We just need to go around to these stores, and to these massive industries in our country, and say, "God sent us by here to say to you that you're not treating his children right. And we've come here to ask you to make the first item on your agenda—fair treatment where God's children are concerned. Now if you are not prepared to do that, we do have an agenda that we must follow. And our agenda calls for withdrawing economic support from you."

22 And so far, as a result of this, we are asking you tonight, to go out and tell your neighbors not to buy Coca-Cola in Memphis. Go by and tell them not to buy Sealtest Milk. Tell them not to buy—what is the other bread?—Wonder Bread. And what is the other bread company, Jesse? Tell them not to buy Hart's Bread. As Jesse Jackson has said, "Up to now, only the garbage men have been feeling pain, now we must kind of redistribute the pain." We are choosing these companies because they haven't been fair in their hiring policies; and we are choosing them because they can begin the **process** of saying they are going to support the needs and the rights of these men who are on strike. And then they can move downtown and tell Mayor Loeb to do what is right.

23 But not only that, we've got to strengthen black institutions. I call upon you to take your money out of the banks downtown and deposit your money in Tri-State Bank. We want a "bank-in" movement in Memphis. Go by the Savings and Loan Association. I'm not asking you something that we don't do ourselves at SCLC. Judge Hooks and others will tell you that we have an account here in the savings and loan association from the Southern Christian Leadership Conference. We are telling you to follow what we are doing. Put your money there. You have six or seven black insurance companies here in the city of Memphis. Take out your insurance there. We want to have an "insurance-in."

24 Now these are some practical things that we can do. We begin the process of building a greater economic **base**. And at the same time, we are putting pressure where it really hurts. I ask you to follow through here.

25 Now, let me say as I move to my conclusion, that we've got to give ourselves to this struggle until the end. Nothing would be more tragic than to stop at this point, in Memphis. We've got to see it through. And when we have our march, you need to be there. If it means leaving work, if it means leaving school—be there. Be concerned about your brother. You may not be on strike. But either we go up together, or we go down together.

26   Let us develop a kind of dangerous unselfishness. One day a man came to Jesus; and he wanted to raise some questions about some vital matters of life. At points, he wanted to trick Jesus, and show him that he knew a little more than Jesus knew, and through this throw him off base. Now that question could have easily ended up in a philosophical and theological debate. But Jesus immediately pulled that question from mid-air, and placed it on a dangerous curve between Jerusalem and Jericho. And he talked about a certain man, who fell among thieves. You remember that a Levite and a priest passed by on the other side. They didn't stop to help him. And finally a man of another race came by. He got down from his beast, decided not to be compassionate by proxy. But he got down with him, administered first aid, and helped the man in need. Jesus ended up saying, "This was the good man, this was the great man, because he had the capacity to project the 'I' into the 'thou,' and to be concerned about his brother" Now you know, we use our imagination a great deal to try to determine why the priest and the Levite didn't stop. At times we say they were busy going to a church meeting—an ecclesiastical gathering—and they had to get on down to Jerusalem so they wouldn't be late for their meeting. At other times we would speculate that there was a religious law that "One who was engaged in religious ceremonials was not to touch a human body twenty-four hours before the ceremony." And every now and then we begin to wonder whether maybe they were not going down to Jerusalem, or down to Jericho, rather to organize a "Jericho Road Improvement Association." That's a possibility. Maybe they felt that it was better to deal with the problem from the causal root, rather than to get bogged down with an individual effect.

27   But I'm going to tell you what my imagination tells me. It's possible that those men were afraid. You see, the Jericho road is a dangerous road. I remember when Mrs. King and I were first in Jerusalem. We rented a car and drove from Jerusalem down to Jericho. And as soon as we got on that road, I said to my wife, "I can see why Jesus used this as the setting for his parable." It's a winding, meandering road. It's really conducive for ambushing. You start out in Jerusalem, which is about 1200 miles, or rather 1200 feet above sea level. And by the time you get down to Jericho, fifteen or twenty minutes later, you're about 2200 feet below sea level. That's a dangerous road. In the days of Jesus it came to be known as the "Bloody Pass." And you know, it's possible that the priest and the Levite looked over that man on the ground and wondered if the robbers were still around. Or it's possible that they felt that the man on the ground was merely faking. And he was acting like he had been robbed and hurt, in order to seize them over there, lure them there for quick and easy seizure. And so the first question that the Priest asked, the first question that the Levite asked was, "If I stop to help this man, what will happen to me?" But then the Good Samaritan came by. And he reversed the question: "If I do not stop to help this man, what will happen to him?"

28   That's the question before you tonight. Not, "If I stop to help the sanitation workers, what will happen to my job." Not, "If I stop to help the sanitation workers what will happen to all of the hours that I usually spend in my office every day and every week as a pastor?" The question is not, "If I stop to help this man in need, what will happen to me?" The question is, "If I do not stop to help the sanitation workers, what will happen to them?" That's the question.

29   Let us rise up tonight with a greater readiness. Let us stand with a greater determination. And let us move on in these powerful days, these days of challenge to make America what it ought to be. We have an opportunity to make America a better nation. And I want to thank God, once more, for allowing me to be here with you.

Skill: Central or Main Idea

Achieving King's goal of universal equality will require determination and unity, two ideas that are emphasized through much of the speech. Here, he asks his audience to rise and stand together to demand equality.

30   You know, several years ago, I was in New York City autographing the first book that I had written. And while sitting there autographing books, a demented black woman came up. The only question I heard from her was, "Are you Martin Luther King?"

31   And I was looking down writing, and I said, "Yes." And the next minute I felt something beating on my chest. Before I knew it I had been stabbed by this demented woman. I was rushed to Harlem Hospital. It was a dark Saturday afternoon. And that blade had gone through, and the X-rays revealed that the tip of the blade was on the edge of my aorta, the main artery. And once that's punctured, you drown in your own blood—that's the end of you.

32   It came out in the *New York Times* the next morning, that if I had merely sneezed, I would have died. Well, about four days later, they allowed me, after the operation, after my chest had been opened, and the blade had been taken out, to move around in the wheel chair in the hospital. They allowed me to read some of the mail that came in, and from all over the states and the world, kind letters came in. I read a few, but one of them I will never forget. I had received one from the President and the Vice-President. I've forgotten what those telegrams said. I'd received a visit and a letter from the Governor of New York, but I've forgotten what that letter said. But there was another letter that came from a little girl, a young girl, who was a student at the White Plains High School. And I looked at that letter, and I'll never forget it. It said simply, "Dear Dr. King, I am a ninth-grade student at the White Plains High School." She said, "While it should not matter, I would like to mention that I'm a white girl. I read in the paper of your misfortune, and of your suffering. And I read that if you had sneezed, you would have died. And I'm simply writing you to say that I'm so happy that you didn't sneeze."

NOTES

Skill:
Rhetoric

King uses the same repeating phrase to emphasize and memorialize the successes of the civil rights movement. The repetition of these accomplishments serves to persuade the audience that victory is possible and to keep fighting.

33 And I want to say tonight—I want to say tonight that I, too, am happy that I didn't sneeze. Because if I had sneezed, I wouldn't have been around here in 1960, when students all over the South started sitting-in at lunch counters. And I knew that as they were sitting in, they were really standing up for the best in the American dream. And taking the whole nation back to those great wells of democracy which were dug deep by the Founding Fathers in the Declaration of Independence and the Constitution. If I had sneezed, I wouldn't have been around here in 1961, when we decided to take a ride for freedom, and ended segregation in interstate travel. If I had sneezed, I wouldn't have been around here in 1962, when Negroes in Albany, Georgia decided to straighten their backs up. And whenever men and women straighten their backs up, they are going somewhere, because a man can't ride your back unless it is bent. If I had sneezed, if I had sneezed, I wouldn't have been here in 1963, when the black people of Birmingham, Alabama aroused the conscience of this nation, and brought into being the Civil Rights Bill. If I had sneezed, I wouldn't have had a chance later that year, in August, to try to tell America about a dream that I had had. If I had sneezed, I wouldn't have been down in Selma, Alabama, to see the great movement there. If I had sneezed, I wouldn't have been in Memphis to see a community rally around those brothers and sisters who are suffering. I'm so happy that I didn't sneeze.

34 And they were telling me, now, it doesn't matter, now. It really doesn't matter what happens now. I left Atlanta this morning, and as we got started on the plane, there were six of us, the pilot said over the public address system, "We are sorry for the delay, but we have Dr. Martin Luther King on the plane. And to be sure that all of the bags were checked, and to be sure that nothing would be wrong on the plane, we had to check out everything carefully. And we've had the plane protected and guarded all night."

35 And then I got into Memphis. And some began to say the threats, or talk about the threats that were out. What would happen to me from some of our sick white brothers?

36 Well, I don't know what will happen now. We've got some difficult days ahead. But it really doesn't matter with me now, because I've been to the mountaintop. And I don't mind. Like anybody, I would like to live a long life. Longevity has its place. But I'm not concerned about that now. I just want to do God's will. And He's allowed me to go up to the mountain. And I've looked over. And I've seen the Promised Land. I may not get there with you. But I want you to know tonight that we, as a people, will get to the promised land. And I'm happy tonight. I'm not worried about anything. I'm not fearing any man. Mine eyes have seen the glory of the coming of the Lord.

Copyright © BookheadEd Learning, LLC

First Read

Read "I've Been to the Mountaintop." After you read, complete the Think Questions below.

☁ THINK QUESTIONS

1. What is "this whole thing about," according to the speaker? Cite evidence from paragraph 10 to support your answer.

2. What specific actions does the speaker propose the audience take in order to exercise their "power of economic withdrawal"? Support your answer with evidence from the text.

3. Citing evidence from the text to support your answer, explain why the speaker tells the parable of the Good Samaritan in "I've Been to the Mountaintop."

4. What is the meaning of the word **vacillating** as it is used in the text? Write your best definition here, along with a brief explanation of how you arrived at its meaning.

5. Read the following dictionary entry:

   base
   base /bās/ *noun*

   1. the bottom part of something that provides structural support
   2. any one of the four stations in a softball or baseball infield
   3. something from which people draw support

   Use context to determine which of these definitions most closely matches the use of **base** in the text. Write the correct definition of *base* here and explain how you figured out its meaning.

Skill:
Central or Main Idea

Use the Checklist to analyze Central or Main Idea in "I've Been to the Mountaintop." Refer to the sample student annotations about Central or Main Idea in the text.

••• CHECKLIST FOR CENTRAL OR MAIN IDEA

In order to identify two or more central ideas of a text, note the following:

✓ the main idea in each paragraph or group of paragraphs

✓ key details in each paragraph or section of text, distinguishing what they have in common

✓ whether the details contain information that could indicate more than one main idea in a text

- A science text, for example, may provide information about a specific environment and also a message on ecological awareness.

- A biography may contain equally important ideas about a person's achievements, influence, and the time period in which the person lives or lived.

✓ when each central idea emerges

✓ ways that the central ideas interact and build on one another

To determine two or more central ideas of a text and analyze their development over the course of the text, including how they interact and build on one another to provide a complex analysis, consider the following questions:

✓ What main idea(s) do the details in each paragraph explain or describe?

✓ What central or main ideas do all the paragraphs support?

✓ How do the central ideas interact and build on one another? How is that affected when they emerge?

✓ How might you provide an objective summary of the text? What details would you include?

Skill:
Central or Main Idea

Reread paragraphs 34–36 of "I've Been to the Mountaintop." Then, using the Checklist on the previous page, answer the multiple-choice questions below.

⟳ YOUR TURN

1. How does sharing the threats he has received help King add to one of the central ideas of the text?

   ○ A. It helps the reader understand that Dr. King is in grave danger and could be harmed.

   ○ B. It strengthens his argument that the path to equality won't be easy, but it is worth it.

   ○ C. It builds on the themes of unity and opportunity, even in times of instability.

   ○ D. It helps strengthen his argument that equal rights should be granted to all Americans.

2. What is the central idea of King's closing paragraph?

   ○ A. That regardless of what happens next, Dr. King has seen what could be and has faith in God that one day African Americans will achieve equality.

   ○ B. That the Promised Land is a place all African Americans will get to no matter what, as King has already been there.

   ○ C. That African Americans should come together to make the world a better place.

   ○ D. That nothing matters to Dr. King now, as he has been to the mountaintop and feels that he is now free.

Skill:
Rhetoric

Use the Checklist to analyze Rhetoric in "I've Been to the Mountaintop." Refer to the sample student annotations about Rhetoric in the text.

••• CHECKLIST FOR RHETORIC

In order to identify a speaker's reasoning, point of view, and use of evidence and rhetoric, note the following:

✓ the stance, or position, the speaker takes on a topic

✓ the use of rhetorical appeals, including appeals to *logos* (logic), *ethos* (trust), and *pathos* (emotions)

✓ the use of rhetorical devices, such as:

- sensory language that appeals to the senses and creates a vivid picture in the minds of readers and listeners

- repetition of the same word or phrase to emphasize an idea or claim. Look for:

  > anaphora, or repetition at the start of a sentence or clause

  > anadiplosis, or repetition of the last word in a sentence or clause

✓ the speaker's choice of words, the points he or she chooses to emphasize, and the tone, or general attitude

To evaluate a speaker's point of view, reasoning, and use of evidence and rhetoric, consider the following questions:

✓ What is the speaker's point of view? Is their stance based on sound, logical reasoning? Why or why not?

✓ Does the speaker use facts and evidence to make a point? Are they exaggerated? How do you know?

✓ Does the speaker use rhetorical devices? If so, are they effective? Why or why not?

✓ What points does the speaker choose to emphasize? How does the speaker's choice of words affect his or her tone?

Skill:
Rhetoric

Reread paragraphs 3–6 of "I've Been to the Mountaintop." Then, using the Checklist on the previous page, answer the multiple-choice questions below.

⟳ YOUR TURN

1. The speaker repeats the phrase "I wouldn't stop there" seven times in paragraphs 3–6. This rhetorical device is called—

   ○ A. the rhetorical appeal known as *pathos*.
   ○ B. anaphora.
   ○ C. rhetorical shift.
   ○ D. antithesis.

2. Which statement best describes the effect of the rhetorical device in question 1 on how the passage is read and understood?

   ○ A. It powerfully calls attention to the progress of human history while creating a personal connection between the speaker and his audience that is intended to convince listeners that remarkable progress is yet to come right there in Memphis.
   ○ B. It reveals that the speaker will soon move on and that the people must commit to carrying on his nonviolent approach to achieving equality for all.
   ○ C. It alerts listeners to the fact that the speaker knows a lot about history and they should be honored that he has come back to Memphis to help fight for workers' rights and civil rights nationwide.
   ○ D. It tells listeners that they should be wary of participating in marches or protests as they are likely to be part of only one small moment in history.

3. The speaker says, "But I know, somehow, that only when it is dark enough can you see the stars." Why does the speaker use the rhetorical device evident in this sentence?

   ○ A. He uses it to change the audience's focus from the historic times he mentioned to the importance of the march that is to take place the next day.
   ○ B. He uses it as a way to logically defend the troubled times in the United States and around the world.
   ○ C. He uses it to help convince the audience to fight for civil rights by describing a figurative contrast between keeping hope in the troubled times they live in.
   ○ D. He uses it to provide proof that nonviolent protests are not always effective and therefore not necessary.

Skill: Language, Style, and Audience

Use the Checklist to analyze Language, Style, and Audience in "I've Been to the Mountaintop." Refer to the sample student annotations about Language, Style, and Audience in the text.

••• CHECKLIST FOR LANGUAGE, STYLE, AND AUDIENCE

In order to determine an author's style and possible intended audience, do the following:

✓ identify instances where the author uses key terms throughout the course of a text

✓ examine surrounding words and phrases to determine the context, connotation, style, and tone of the term

✓ analyze how the author's treatment of the key term affects the reader's understanding of the text

✓ note the audience—both intended and unintended—and possible reactions to the author's word choice, style, and treatment of key terms

To analyze how an author's treatment of language and key terms affect the reader's understanding of the text, consider the following questions:

✓ How do the author's word choices enhance or change what is being described?

✓ How do the author's word choices affect the reader's understanding of key terms and ideas in the text?

✓ How do choices about language affect the author's style and audience?

✓ How often does the author use this term or terms?

Skill: Language, Style, and Audience

Reread paragraphs 32 and 33 of "I've Been to the Mountaintop." Then, using the Checklist on the previous page, answer the multiple-choice questions below.

⟳ YOUR TURN

1. How does the repetition of the phrase "if I had sneezed" enhance the meaning of these paragraphs?

   ○ A. It emphasizes that King is excited about the next chapter of the civil rights movement.
   ○ B. It enhances the reader's understanding of how King felt happy to be alive.
   ○ C. It emphasizes that King is proud and feels lucky to have been part of many great moments in the civil rights struggle.
   ○ D. It enhances the reader's understanding of the impact of the events of the civil rights movement that occurred over the years.

2. What is the effect of this summary of successes on the audience?

   ○ A. It reminds the audience of the gradual progress that has been made, which inspires action, hope, and the need to keep fighting.
   ○ B. It teaches the audience about the major events of the civil rights movement.
   ○ C. It helps the reader understand how close King was to dying and how happy he is to be alive.
   ○ D. It builds tension by foreshadowing King's assassination.

Please note that excerpts and passages in the StudySync® library and this workbook are intended as touchstones to generate interest in an author's work. The excerpts and passages do not substitute for the reading of entire texts, and StudySync® strongly recommends that students seek out and purchase the whole literary or informational work in order to experience it as the author intended. Links to online resellers are available in our digital library. In addition, complete works may be ordered through an authorized reseller by filling out and returning to StudySync® the order form enclosed in this workbook.

Reading & Writing Companion   111

Close Read

Reread "I've Been to the Mountaintop." As you reread, complete the Skills Focus questions below. Then use your answers and annotations from the questions to help you complete the Write activity.

◎ SKILLS FOCUS

1. What is one of King's central or main ideas in this text? Support your answer with textual evidence.

2. Identify a passage in "I've Been to the Mountaintop" that reveals the audience of the speech. Analyze how King communicates his purpose to this audience.

3. Highlight a rhetorical device that King uses in his speech. Then, analyze the effect the rhetorical devices have on the way the text is read and understood.

4. Identify an example in the text where King urges his audience to partake in nonviolent forms of resistance. Explain why you believe nonviolence is important for King in the fight for equality.

✎ WRITE

RHETORICAL ANALYSIS: What makes rhetoric effective? Identify King's main idea and purpose in this speech. Then discuss what aspect of King's rhetoric is most crucial to convincing his audience of his main idea. Cite examples of rhetoric from the text and explain how they are used to support King's central idea.

Extended Writing Project and Grammar

EXTENDED WRITING PROJECT

ARGUMENTATIVE WRITING

Argumentative Writing Process: Plan

PLAN	DRAFT	REVISE	EDIT AND PUBLISH

John Green once said that he defines success by asking himself, "What did I learn?" and "Who did it help?" Many authors in this unit argue what success in pursuit of their goals, or winning, means to them—at the workplace, in the classroom, or even in life itself. For some, winning means achieving a hard-earned victory or achieving a certain economic status. For others, winning carries an altruistic meaning, working towards equity for others or having the integrity to forsake political power.

WRITING PROMPT

How do we define success?

Write an essay in which you argue what success really means. What does it mean to "win"? What are the benefits of winning? What are the costs? Write a clear, arguable thesis, and use evidence from at least two texts in the unit to support your argument. You may also draw on relevant personal experiences to support your ideas. Remember to include the following in your argumentative essay:

- an introduction
- a thesis statement
- coherent body paragraphs
- supporting evidence and original commentary
- a counterargument
- a conclusion

Writing to Sources

As you gather ideas and information from the texts in the unit, be sure to:

- include a claim,
- address counterarguments,
- use evidence from multiple sources, and
- avoid overly relying on one source.

Introduction to Argumentative Writing

Argumentative writing aims to persuade an audience to agree with a writer's point of view on a topic or issue. In an argumentative essay, a writer states a claim and then provides facts, details, examples, and quotations to support it. Strong argumentative writing effectively uses genre characteristics and craft such as relevant evidence, and a clear organizational structure to persuade readers to accept and agree with the writer's claim. The characteristics of argumentative writing include:

- an introduction

- a thesis statement

- evidence

- transitions

- a conclusion

In addition to these characteristics, argumentative writers also carefully craft their work through their use of a clear and persuasive organizational structure as well as counterarguments and a strong, confident tone. These choices help make the text more persuasive. Effective arguments combine these genre characteristics and craft to engage and convince the reader.

As you continue with this Extended Writing Project, you'll receive more instruction and practice in crafting each of the characteristics of argumentative writing to create your own argumentative essay.

Please note that excerpts and passages in the StudySync® library and this workbook are intended as touchstones to generate interest in an author's work. The excerpts and passages do not substitute for the reading of entire texts, and StudySync® strongly recommends that students seek out and purchase the whole literary or informational work in order to experience it as the author intended. Links to online resellers are available in our digital library. In addition, complete works may be ordered through an authorized reseller by filling out and returning to StudySync® the order form enclosed in this workbook.

Reading & Writing Companion

115

Before you get started on your own argumentative essay, read this essay that one student, Alex, wrote in response to the writing prompt. As you read the Model, highlight and annotate the features of argumentative writing that Alex included in his essay.

NOTES

≡ STUDENT MODEL

Champions of Change

1   When you envision "winning," you might see a runner crossing a finish line with his or her arms extended into the air. Perhaps you visualize the first-place winner of a science fair holding a gold medal with a confident smile. Wins such as these are personal achievements. Individual wins are certainly worthy of praise, but they do not embody what success really means. A true winner takes courageous action and, through his or her fortitude, inspires a series of incremental achievements toward a future goal. This courageous action can take many forms. The decision in the Supreme Court case *Brown v. Board of Education* and George Marshall's speech at Harvard University demonstrate how speakers and writers use words to publicly express ideals. These texts show that winning can mean the courageous act of publicly declaring a need for change in society.

2   In 1951, Oliver Brown's daughter, Linda, was denied entry into Topeka, Kansas's all-white elementary schools on the basis of the "separate but equal" doctrine. The doctrine was set in place in 1896 after the verdict in *Plessy v. Ferguson* legalized racial segregation of public facilities ("Documents Related to Brown v. Board of Education"). In practice, the separate facilities were not actually equal. Schools for African American students received significantly less funding than white schools did ("*Brown v. Board at Fifty*"). After decades of mandated segregation, Oliver Brown, along with others seeking justice, filed a class action suit against the city's board of education. They claimed that segregated schools violated the Fourteenth Amendment, or the right to equal protection under the law ("Documents Related to Brown v. Board of Education"). The children and families who risked their lives to go to school and the lawyers who stuck with the case combined their efforts in defense of African Americans' access to education and, more broadly, their civil rights.

3   The case made it to the Supreme Court of the United States, and in 1952, the justices unanimously ruled that segregation in schools was unconstitutional. Chief Justice Warren opens the decision by stating, "We cannot turn the clock back" and "We must consider public education in the light of its full development and its present place in American life throughout the Nation." Warren's references to time serve multiple purposes. First, he states the simple truth that the past cannot not be changed. Then, by saying, "in the light of its full development," he implies that public education has transformed over time. Life in mid-twentieth century America differed from how it was in "1868, when the [Fourteenth] Amendment was adopted." Yet, by 1952, many people had grown accustomed to segregational practices. The Supreme Court justices challenge this way of thinking by acknowledging that change in this country is inevitable. Thus, it was necessary to honor this inevitability by re-evaluating public education and the laws that regulate it in the present.

4   The decision of the court goes on to demonstrate that the doctrine of "separate but equal" is unequal because it "generates a feeling of inferiority" in African American students. The laws mandated by *Plessy v. Ferguson* had great influence over American life. By declaring "separate but equal" as "inherently unequal," the court risked inciting outrage, but made the determination that they felt was right. Many of those who benefited from segregation did not want it to change. Nonetheless, the justices fulfilled their role of interpreting the law through the Constitution. With this landmark case, the Supreme Court reminded citizens that their way of life can and will evolve. The language in the Supreme Court's verdict further encouraged people to question the legality of segregation in general. The court's bold decision was a win because it motivated more people to continue to fight for civil rights and greater equality on a larger scale. As the ACLU stated upon the 50th anniversary of the decision, Brown v. Board of Education changed America "as a nation, and for the better, and as a result African Americans made tremendous gains in access to education, income, and civic participation, out of which grew a generation of black middle-class leaders in all spheres of our nation's life."

5   George Marshall also uses the power of words to inspire change. Unlike the United States Supreme Court justices who rely on the

clarity of their reasoning to make a point, Marshall uses an emotional appeal to generate meaning, make a point, and persuade his audience in his speech about rebuilding Europe after World War II. Marshall, who was appointed to the position of Secretary of State by President Truman, delivered a commencement address at Harvard University after the Paris Peace Treaties were signed in 1947. In the speech's first sentences, Marshall says, ". . . the world situation is very serious." Here, the author is laying out the purpose for delivering his speech: although the United States and its allies have sacrificed much to win the war, peace cannot be ensured while Europe is on the brink of chaos. Marshall makes a stirring case for the United States to aid their former enemies, and he starts by showing just how high the stakes are for Europe and the world.

6   Marshall then sets out to describe the problem in economic terms and appeal to the patriotic values of his audience. He explains how the Nazi state incorporated the entire German economy into the war effort, disrupting the normal flow of goods between farmers and city dwellers. Marshall argues that unless the United States intervenes, "there can be no political stability and no assured peace." Although Americans may be weary from war, the fight must continue. Marshall charges his audience to continue the war, stating that the United States has a "vast responsibility which history has clearly placed upon our country." With financial assistance from the United States, Europe can re-emerge from devastation. The use of an emotional appeal throughout the speech reminds the audience that the United States is uniquely positioned to champion the rise of free and democratic nations.

7   Marshall had a long history with the European theater before he gave this speech. A five-star general during World War II, Marshall was the creator of the strategy that achieved military victory ("History of the Marshall Plan"). However, he was was convinced that there could be no triumph with Europe in ruins. In its weakened state, it was prey to Russia and communist ideas ("History of the Marshall Plan"). Consequently, the only way the United States could truly win was to assist Europe in recovering politically through economic revitalization. Winning the war for capitalism and free trade meant further sacrifice.

8   Some might say that the mere act of expressing ideas in public hardly constitutes winning, particularly if those words do not incite immediate change. To illustrate, George Marshall's audience was recent Harvard graduates and their families. One might argue that there is no win gained from this speech and that, ultimately, his audience had limited control over the US's aid to foreign countries. This however, misses the purpose of the speech. Marshall may have shared his thinking to an audience at Harvard, but he used this speech to publicly launch his plan for recovery with the full backing of the US State Department. Furthermore, it is important to consider that lasting change rarely happens overnight. Instead, it takes the combined effort of focused leaders like George Marshall to rally others around their vision for progress. Winning comes not just from the final outcome but from the allies and partners gained along the way.

9   When writers make a declaration that challenges the status quo, they put their reputations on the line. They make themselves a target for ridicule and risk alienation. The Supreme Court knew the implications of their verdict. They knew that their decision went against many people's core beliefs. Nevertheless, they made a choice in support of those fighting for civil rights and kick-started a series of changes to American life. Likewise, George Marshall was well aware of the fact that his speech about rebuilding Europe— especially Germany— might be met with resistance, but he continued to move forward with his plans, garnering national attention and international assistance. When writers go against the grain, they can influence more people to share their opinions. Through their declarations, they exhibit the fortitude required to enact change. Courageous writers like Chief Justice Earl Warren and George Marshall embody what it means to win because they effectively challenged entrenched mindsets, inspired their audiences, and built momentum for further growth and change.

Please note that excerpts and passages in the StudySync® library and this workbook are intended as touchstones to generate interest in an author's work. The excerpts and passages do not substitute for the reading of entire texts, and StudySync® strongly recommends that students seek out and purchase the whole literary or informational work in order to experience it as the author intended. Links to online resellers are available in our digital library. In addition, complete works may be ordered through an authorized reseller by filling out and returning to StudySync® the order form enclosed in this workbook.

Reading & Writing
Companion   119

NOTES

Works Cited

"Brown v. Board at Fifty: 'With an Even Hand': A Century of Racial Segregation, 1849–1950." The Library of Congress. www.loc.gov/exhibits/brown/brown-segregation.html#obj20. Accessed 9 November 2019.

"Documents Related to Brown v. Board of Education: Background." U.S. National Archives and Records Administration, 15 August 2016. www.archives.gov/education/lessons/brown-v-board. Accessed 9 November 2019.

"History of the Marshall Plan." The George C. Marshall Foundation. https://www.marshallfoundation.org/marshall/the-marshall-plan/history-marshall-plan/. Accessed 9 November 2019.

✎ WRITE

Writers often take notes about essay ideas before they sit down to write. Think about what you've learned so far about organizing argumentative writing to help you begin prewriting.

- **Purpose:** What does it mean to win? How do the texts support your argument?

- **Audience:** Who is your audience? How do you want them to view the texts differently?

- **Introduction:** How will you introduce the topic and thesis of your essay? Do your topic and thesis present a unique perspective on the texts?

- **Thesis Statement:** What is your claim about the topic or issue? How can you word your claim so it is clear to readers?

- **Evidence:** What evidence will you use to support your claim? What facts, details, examples, and quotations will persuade your audience to agree with your claim?

- **Transitions:** How will you smoothly transition from one idea to another within and across paragraphs?

- **Conclusion:** How will you wrap up your argument? How can you rephrase the main ideas in your argument without being redundant?

Response Instructions

Use the questions in the bulleted list to write a one-paragraph summary. Your summary should describe what you will argue in your argumentative essay like the one above.

Don't worry about including all of the details now; focus only on the most essential and important elements. You will refer to this short summary as you continue through the steps of the writing process.

Please note that excerpts and passages in the StudySync® library and this workbook are intended as touchstones to generate interest in an author's work. The excerpts and passages do not substitute for the reading of entire texts, and StudySync® strongly recommends that students seek out and purchase the whole literary or informational work in order to experience it as the author intended. Links to online resellers are available in our digital library. In addition, complete works may be ordered through an authorized reseller by filling out and returning to StudySync® the order form enclosed in this workbook.

Reading & Writing Companion   **121**

Skill:
Thesis Statement

••• CHECKLIST FOR THESIS STATEMENT

Before you begin writing your thesis statement, ask yourself the following questions:

- What is the prompt asking me to write about?
- What claim do I want to make about the topic of this essay?
- Is my claim precise and informative? Is it specific to my topic? How does it inform the reader about my topic?
- Does my thesis statement introduce the body of my essay?
- Where should I place my thesis statement?

Here are some methods for introducing and developing a topic as well as a precise and informative claim:

- think about the central claim of your essay
  - > identify a clear claim you want to introduce, thinking about:
    - o how closely your claim is related to your topic and how specific it is to your supporting details
    - o how your claim includes necessary information to guide the reader through your argument
- your thesis statement should:
  - > let the reader anticipate the content of your essay
  - > help you begin your essay in an organized manner
  - > present your opinion clearly
  - > respond completely to the writing prompt
- consider the best placement for your thesis statement
  - > if your response is short, you may want to get right to the point and present your thesis statement in the first sentence
  - > if your response is longer (as in a formal essay), you can build up to your thesis statement and place it at the end of your introductory paragraph

---

⟳ YOUR TURN

Read the thesis statements below. Then, complete the chart by sorting the statements into two categories: effective thesis statements and ineffective thesis statements. Write the corresponding letter for each statement in the appropriate column.

	Thesis Statements
A	In his speech at Harvard University, George Marshall uses emotional appeals to generate sympathy and convince America to help its former enemies.
B	George Marshall's speech was a response to the Paris Peace Treaties in 1947.
C	References to similar cases such as *Sweatt v. Painter* are what ultimately convince the reader of the Supreme Court's claim about segregation in *Brown v. Board of Education*.
D	In the verdict of *Brown v. Board of Education*, the Supreme Court determined that segregation is detrimental to African American students.

Effective Thesis Statements	Ineffective Thesis Statements

✎ WRITE

Follow the steps in the checklist to draft a thesis statement for your argumentative essay.

Please note that excerpts and passages in the StudySync® library and this workbook are intended as touchstones to generate interest in an author's work. The excerpts and passages do not substitute for the reading of entire texts, and StudySync® strongly recommends that students seek out and purchase the whole literary or informational work in order to experience it as the author intended. Links to online resellers are available in our digital library. In addition, complete works may be ordered through an authorized reseller by filling out and returning to StudySync® the order form enclosed in this workbook.

Reading & Writing Companion **123**

Skill: Organizing Argumentative Writing

••• CHECKLIST FOR ORGANIZING ARGUMENTATIVE WRITING

As you consider how to organize your writing for your argumentative essay, use the following questions as a guide:

- What evidence can I find that would support my claim?
- What information can I look for to establish the significance of my claim?
- What approach can I use to distinguish my claim from any alternate or opposing claims?
- Did I choose an organizing structure that establishes clear relationships between claims and evidence?

Follow these steps to organize your argumentative essay in a way that logically sequences claim(s), counterclaims, reasons, and evidence:

- identify your precise, or specific, claim or claims and the evidence that supports them
- establish the significance of your claim
  - > find what others may have written about the topic, and learn why they feel it is important
- distinguish the claim or claims from alternate or opposing claims
- find evidence that distinguishes counterclaims from your own claim
- choose an organizing structure that logically sequences and establishes clear relationships between claims and the evidence presented to support the claims

YOUR TURN

Read the thesis statements below. Then, choose the organizational structure that would be most appropriate for the purpose, topic, and context of the corresponding essay, as well as the audience, and write it in the chart.

Organizational Structure Options			
cause and effect	list advantages and disadvantages	problem and solution	compare and contrast

Thesis Statement	Organizational Structure
Eliminating the use of electronics before going to bed is the most effective method for resolving frequent nightmares.	
The benefits of remodeling the college's library outweigh the cost of construction.	
If people did not obey traffic laws, there would be chaos on the roads.	
Homeschooled students and students who attend school on a campus have more in common than most people may think.	

Please note that excerpts and passages in the StudySync® library and this workbook are intended as touchstones to generate interest in an author's work. The excerpts and passages do not substitute for the reading of entire texts, and StudySync® strongly recommends that students seek out and purchase the whole literary or informational work in order to experience it as the author intended. Links to online resellers are available in our digital library. In addition, complete works may be ordered through an authorized reseller by filling out and returning to StudySync® the order form enclosed in this workbook.

Reading & Writing Companion

125

⟳ YOUR TURN

Complete the outline by writing an introductory statement, thesis statement, three main ideas for body paragraphs, and concluding ideas for your argumentative essay. Make sure your ideas are appropriate for the purpose, topic, and context of your essay, as well as your audience.

Outline	Summary
Introductory Statement	
Thesis	
Main Idea 1	
Main Idea 2	
Main Idea 3 (present and refute counterargument)	
Conclusion	

Skill: Reasons and Relevant Evidence

Copyright © BookheadEd Learning, LLC

••• CHECKLIST FOR REASONS AND RELEVANT EVIDENCE

As you determine the reasons and relevant evidence you will need to support your claim, use the following questions as a guide:

- What is my claim (or claims)? What are the strengths and limitations of my claim(s)?

- What relevant evidence do I have? Where could I add more support for my claim(s)?

- What do I know about the audience's:

  > knowledge about my topic?

  > concerns and values?

  > possible biases toward the subject matter?

Use the following steps to help you develop claims fairly and thoroughly:

- establish a claim and counterclaim, which is another claim that attempts to disprove the opposing opinion. Then, evaluate:

  > how precise, specific, and clear the claim and counterclaim are

  > the strengths and limitations of both

  > any biases you have toward both

  > any gaps in support for your claim, so that your support can be more thorough

- consider your audience and their perspective on your topic. Determine:

  > their probable prior knowledge about the topic

  > their concerns and values

  > any biases they may have toward the subject matter

  > how you will need to approach your claim to accommodate your audience

- find the most relevant evidence that supports the claim

⟳ YOUR TURN

Read each quotation from *Brown v. Board of Education* below. Then, complete the chart by sorting the quotations into two categories: those that are relevant and those that are not relevant to the writing topic of "Why segregated public schools are detrimental to a student's ability to learn." Write the corresponding letter for each quotation in the appropriate column.

Quotations	
A	"education is perhaps the most important function of state and local governments"
B	"the policy of separating the races is usually interpreted as denoting the inferiority of the negro group"
C	"a feeling of inferiority . . . may affect their hearts and minds in a way unlikely ever to be undone"
D	"Any language in *Plessy v. Ferguson* contrary to this finding is rejected."

Relevant to Topic	Not Relevant to Topic

⟳ YOUR TURN

Complete the chart below by identifying evidence from each text you've chosen. Identifying evidence will help you support your thesis. Then, explain why this evidence is relevant to your thesis.

Text	Relevant Evidence	Explanation

Argumentative Writing Process: Draft

PLAN	DRAFT	REVISE	EDIT AND PUBLISH

You have already made progress toward writing your argumentative essay. Now it is time to draft your argumentative essay.

✏ WRITE

Use your plan and other responses in your Binder to draft your argumentative essay. You may also have new ideas as you begin drafting. Feel free to explore those new ideas as you have them. You can also ask yourself these questions to ensure that your writing is focused, organized, and developed:

Draft Checklist:

☐ **Focused:** Have I introduced my claim clearly in a thesis statement? Have I included only relevant evidence to support my claim and nothing extraneous that might confuse my readers?

☐ **Organized:** Have I organized my analysis in a way that makes sense? Have I established clear relationships among claims, counterclaims, reasons, and evidence?

☐ **Developed:** Have I clearly stated reasons that support my claim? Have I identified counterclaims in a way my audience can follow? Is my evidence sufficient?

Please note that excerpts and passages in the StudySync® library and this workbook are intended as touchstones to generate interest in an author's work. The excerpts and passages do not substitute for the reading of entire texts, and StudySync® strongly recommends that students seek out and purchase the whole literary or informational work in order to experience it as the author intended. Links to online resellers are available in our digital library. In addition, complete works may be ordered through an authorized reseller by filling out and returning to StudySync® the order form enclosed in this workbook.

Reading & Writing Companion   **129**

Here is Alex's argumentative essay draft. As you read, notice how Alex develops his draft to be focused, organized, and developed.

NOTES

Skill:
Introductions

After discussing his introduction with a partner, Alex understands that he needs to add a more interesting "hook." He decides to provide some examples of winning that his reader will be able to envision. Alex also adds clarifying language about individual wins and adjusts his thesis to be more specific, including the words *courageous* and *publicly*.

STUDENT MODEL: FIRST DRAFT

Student Model: First Draft

1   ~~There are lots of ways to win, such as winning a race or a science fair. Wins such as these are isolated achievements. Individual wins are certainly worthy of prase. A true winner takes courageous action and, through his or her fortitude, inspires a series of incremental achievements toward a future goal. This courageous act can take many forms as seen in the decision in the Supreme Court case Brown v. Board of Education and George Marshall's speech at Harvard University demonstrate how speakers and writers use words to publicly express ideals. These texts show that winning can mean the act of declaring a need for change in society.~~

When you envision "winning," you might see a runner crossing a finish line with his or her arms extended into the air. Perhaps you visualize the first-place winner of a science fair holding a gold medal with a confident smile. Wins such as these are personal achievements. Individual wins are certainly worthy of praise, but they do not embody what success really means. A true winner takes courageous action and, through his or her fortitude, inspires a series of incremental achievements toward a future goal. This courageous action can take many forms. The decision in the Supreme Court case *Brown v. Board of Education* and George Marshall's speech at Harvard University demonstrate how speakers and writers use words to publicly express ideals. These texts show that winning can mean the courageous act of publicly declaring a need for change in society.

2   In 1951, Oliver Brown's daughter, Linda, was denied entry into Topeka, Kansas's all-white elementary schools on the basis of the "separate but equal" doctrine. The doctrine was set in place in 1896 after the verdict in *Plessy v. Ferguson* legalized racial segregation of public facilities ("Documents Related to *Brown v. Board of Education*"). In practice, the separate facilities were not actually equal. Schools for African American students received significantly less funding than white schools did ("*Brown v. Board at Fifty*"). After decades of

NOTES

mandated segregation, Oliver Brown, along with others seeking justice, filed a class action suit against the city's board of education. They claimed that segregated schools violated the Fourteenth Amendment, or the right to equal protection under the law ("Documents Related to *Brown v. Board of Education*"). The children and families who risked their lives to go to school and the lawyers who stuck with the case combined their efforts in defense of African Americans' access to education and, more broadly, their civil rights.

3   In 1952, the justices unanimously ruled that segregation in schools was unconstitutional. Chief Justice Warren opens the decision by stating, "We cannot turn the clock back" and "We must consider public education in the light of its full development and its present place in American life throughout the Nation." Warren's references to time serve multiple purposes. First, he states the simple truth that the past cannot not be changed. Then, by saying, "in the light of its full development," he implies that public education has transformed over time. Life in mid-twentieth century America differed from how it was in "1868, when the [Fourteenth] Amendment was adopted." Yet, by 1952, many people had grown accustomed to segregational practices. The Supreme Court justices challenge this way of thinking by acknowledging that change in this country is inevitable. Thus, it was necessary to honor this inevitability by re-evaluating public education and the laws that regulate it in the present.

4   The decision of the court goes on to demonstrate that the doctrine of "separate but equal" is unequal because it "generates a feeling of inferiority" in African American students. The laws mandated by *Plessy v. Ferguson* had great influence over American life. By declaring "separate but equal" as "inherently unequal," the court risked inciting outrage but made the determination that they felt was right. Many of those who benefited from segregation did not want it to change. Nonetheless, the justices fulfilled their role of interpreting the law through the Constitution. With this landmark case, the Supreme Court reminded citizens that their way of life can and will evolve. The language in the Supreme Court's verdict further encouraged people to question the legality of segregation in general. The court's bold decision was a win because it motivated more people to continue to fight for civil rights and greater equality on a larger scale. As the ACLU stated upon the 50th anniversary of the decision, *Brown v Board of Education* changed America "as a

NOTES

Skill:
Transitions

Alex revisits the checklist and realizes that the relationships between his ideas are not always clear. Alex reviews a list of transition words and adds phrases and words such as *however* and *consequently* to improve the flow and clarify the meaning of his paragraph.

nation, and for the better, and as a result African Americans made tremendous gains in access to education, income, and civic participation, out of which grew a generation of black middle-class leaders in all spheres of our nation's life."

5 George Marshall also uses the power of words to inspire change. Unlike the United States Supreme Court justisses who rely on the clarity of their reasoning to make a point, Marshall uses an emotional appeal to generate meaning, make a point, and persuades his audience in his speech about rebuilding Europe after World War II. Marshall, appointed to the position of Secretary of State by President Truman, delivered a commencement address at Harvard University. In the speech's first sentences, Marshall says, "the world situation is very serious." Here, the author is laying out the purpose for delivering his speech. He argues that the United States and its allies have sacrificed much to win the war, peace cannot be ensured while Europe is on the brink of chaos. Marshall makes a stirring case for the United States to aid their former enemies. He starts by showing just how high the stakes are for Europe and the world.

6 Marshall then sets out to describe the problem in economic terms and appeal to the patriotic values of his audience. He explains how the Nazi state incorporated the entire German economy into the war effort, disrupting the normal flow of goods between farmers and city dwellers. Marshall argues that unless the United States intervenes, "there can be no political stability and no assured peace." Although Americans may be tired from war, the fight must continue. Marshall charges his audience to continue the war, stating that the United States has a "vast responsibility which history has clearly placed upon our country." With financial assistance from the United States, Europe can come out from devastation.

7 ~~Marshall had a long history with the European theater before he gave this speech. Marshall was a five-star general during World War II. He created the strategy that achieved military victory ("History of the Marshall Plan"). Marshall was convinced that there could be no triumph with Europe in ruins. In its weakened state, it was prey to Russia and communist ideas ("History of the Marshall Plan). The only way the United States could truly win was to assist Europe in recovering politically through economic revitalization. Winning the war for capitalism and free trade meant further sacrifice.~~

Marshall had a long history with the European theater before he gave this speech. A five-star general during World War II, Marshall was the creator of the strategy that achieved military victory ("History of the Marshall Plan"). However, he was was convinced that there could be no triumph with Europe in ruins. In its weakened state, it was prey to Russia and communist ideas ("History of the Marshall Plan). Consequently, the only way the United States could truly win was to assist Europe in recovering politically through economic revitalization. Winning the war for capitalism and free trade meant further sacrifice.

8   Some might say that the mere act of sharing one's ideals publicly doesn't really count as winning, particularly if those words don't work right away. For example, George Marshall presented his speech to a group of recent Harvard graduates and their families. One might argue that there is no win gained from this speech and that those people had no control of the U.S.'s aid to foreign countries. Marshall may have shared his thinking to an audience at Harvard, but he was the secretary of state. He just used this opportunity to tell the public about his ideas. He just used this opportunity to tell the public about his ideas. Also, lasting change rarely happens overnight. Instead, it takes the combined effort of focused leaders these to rally others around their vision for progress. Winning comes not just from the final outcome but from the allies and partners gained along the way.

9   ~~When writers make a declaration that challenges the status quo, they put their reputations on the line. They make themselves a target for ridicule, being alienated, and discrimination. The Supreme Court knew the implications of their verdict. They knew that their decision went against many people's core beliefs. Nevertheless, they made a choice in support of those fighting for civil rights and kick started a series of changes to American life. When writers go against the grain they can influence more people to share their opinions through their declarations, these texts exemplify the fortitude required to enact change.~~

When writers make a declaration that challenges the status quo, they put their reputations on the line. They make themselves a target for ridicule and risk alienation. The Supreme Court knew the

NOTES

Skill:
Conclusions

Alex realizes he didn't include any summarizing thoughts for "The Marshall Plan Speech." He also notices that his final sentence could better capture his thesis, and he believes he can further improve his essay by leaving readers with a memorable final idea. He adds a reference to "The Marshall Plan Speech" to the conclusion and writes an additional closing sentence to more meaningfully capture his thesis.

implications of their verdict. They knew that their decision went against many people's core beliefs. Nevertheless, they made a choice in support of those fighting for civil rights and kick-started a series of changes to American life. Likewise, George Marshall was well aware of the fact that his speech about rebuilding Europe— especially Germany— might be met with resistance, but he continued to move forward with his plans, garnering national attention and international assistance. When writers go against the grain, they can influence more people to share their opinions. Through their declarations, they exhibit the fortitude required to enact change. Courageous writers like Chief Justice Earl Warren and George Marshall embody what it means to win because they effectively challenged entrenched mindsets, inspired their audiences, and built momentum for further growth and change.

Skill:
Introductions

••• CHECKLIST FOR INTRODUCTIONS

Before you write your introduction, ask yourself the following questions:

- What is my claim? In addition:

  > Do I state my claim in a clear and powerful thesis statement?

  > How can I make my claim more precise and informative?

  > Have I included why my claim is significant to discuss?

- How can I introduce my topic? Have I organized complex ideas, concepts, and information so that each new element builds on the previous element and creates a unified whole?

- How will I "hook" my reader's interest? I might:

  > start with an attention-grabbing statement

  > begin with an intriguing question

  > use descriptive words to set a scene

Below are two strategies to help you introduce your precise claim and topic clearly in an introduction:

- Peer Discussion

  > Talk about your topic with a partner, explaining what you already know and your ideas about your topic.

  > Write notes about the ideas you have discussed and any new questions you may have.

  > Review your notes, and think about what your claim or controlling idea will be.

  > Write a possible "hook."

- Freewriting

  > Freewrite for 10 minutes about your topic. Don't worry about grammar, punctuation, or having fully formed ideas. The point of freewriting is to discover ideas.

  > Review your notes, and think about what your claim or controlling idea will be.

  > Write a possible "hook."

YOUR TURN

Choose the best answer to each question.

1. Which of the following elements belongs in an introductory paragraph?

   ○ A. a counterargument with supporting evidence
   ○ B. a list of reasons to support a claim
   ○ C. relevant evidence to justify a claim
   ○ D. a thesis statement containing a claim

2. The following introduction is from a previous draft of Alex's essay. Alex needs to add a hook to grab his audience's attention and introduce his topic. Which sentence could he add to achieve this goal?

   > A true winner takes courageous action and, through his or her fortitude, inspires a series of incremental achievements toward a future goal. This courageous act can take many forms. The decision in the Supreme Court case *Brown v. Board of Education* and George Marshall's speech at Harvard University demonstrate how speakers and writers use words to publicly express their ideals. These texts show that winning can mean the act of declaring a need for change in society.

   ○ A. The texts in this unit portrayed a range of individual experiences.
   ○ B. Have you ever wondered what makes someone a winner? Is it individual victory? Or personal growth? Or is it something more complex?
   ○ C. "The Marshall Plan Speech" was written to spark change in society.
   ○ D. The texts I will discuss cover a variety of arguments and points of view.

✎ **WRITE**

Use the checklist to revise the introduction of your argumentative essay.

Skill:
Transitions

••• CHECKLIST FOR TRANSITIONS

Before you revise your current draft to include transitions, think about:

- the key ideas you discuss in your body paragraphs
- the relationships among your claim(s), reasons, and evidence
- the relationship between your claim(s) and counterclaims
- the logical progression of your argument

Next, reread your current draft and note places in your essay where:

- the relationships among your claim(s), counterclaims, and reasons and evidence are unclear
- you could add linking words, vary sentence structure, or use other transitional devices to make your argument more cohesive. Look for:

  > sudden jumps in your ideas

  > breaks between paragraphs where the ideas in the next paragraph do not logically follow from the points in the previous paragraph

  > repetitive sentence structures

Revise your draft to use words, phrases, and clauses as well as varied syntax to link the major sections of your essay, create cohesion, and clarify the relationships between claim(s) and reasons, between reasons and evidence, and between claim(s) and counterclaims, using the following questions as a guide:

- Are there unifying relationships among the claims, reasons, and evidence I present in my argument?
- How do my claim(s) and counterclaim(s) relate?
- Have I made these relationships clear?
- How can I link major sections of my essay using words, phrases, clauses, and varied syntax?

Please note that excerpts and passages in the StudySync® library and this workbook are intended as touchstones to generate interest in an author's work. The excerpts and passages do not substitute for the reading of entire texts, and StudySync® strongly recommends that students seek out and purchase the whole literary or informational work in order to experience it as the author intended. Links to online resellers are available in our digital library. In addition, complete works may be ordered through an authorized reseller by filling out and returning to StudySync® the order form enclosed in this workbook.

Reading & Writing Companion   137

⟳ YOUR TURN

Choose the best answer to each question.

1. Below is a passage from the next draft of Alex's essay. The connection between the ideas in the underlined sentence is unclear. What transition should Alex use to replace *and* after "The court's bold decision was a win" to make his writing more coherent?

> Nonetheless, the justices fulfilled their role of interpreting the law through the constitution. With this landmark case, the Supreme Court reminded citizens that their way of life can and will evolve. The language in the Supreme Court's verdict encouraged people to question the legality of segregation in general. <u>The court's bold decision was a win and the decision motivated more people to continue to fight for civil rights and greater equality on a larger scale.</u>

- ○ A. another key point
- ○ B. in the final analysis
- ○ C. because
- ○ D. prior to

2. Below is a passage from a previous draft of Alex's essay. Alex did not use an appropriate transition to show the relationship between the ideas in sentences 1 and 2. In sentence 2, which of the following transitions is the best replacement for *Conversely*?

> (1) Some might say that the mere act of expressing ideas in public hardly constitutes winning, particularly if those words do not incite immediate change. (2) Conversely, George Marshall delivered his speech at a small lunch to thirteen Harvard graduates. (3) One might argue that there is no win gained from this speech and that, ultimately, his audience had no control over the U.S.'s aid to foreign countries.

- ○ A. Eventually
- ○ B. To illustrate
- ○ C. Consequently
- ○ D. On balance

✏ WRITE

Use the questions in the checklist to revise your use of transitions in a section of your argumentative essay.

Skill:
Conclusions

••• CHECKLIST FOR CONCLUSIONS

Before you write your conclusion, ask yourself the following questions:

- How can I rephrase the thesis or main idea?
- How can I write my conclusion so that it supports and follows from the information I presented?
- How can I communicate the importance of my topic? What information do I need?

Below are two strategies to help you provide a concluding statement or section that follows from and supports the information or explanation you presented:

- Peer Discussion

  > After you have written your introduction and body paragraphs, talk with a partner about what you want readers to remember, writing notes about your discussion.

  > Think about how you can articulate, or express, the significance of your topic in the conclusion.

  > Rephrase your main idea to show the depth of your knowledge and support for the information you presented.

  > Write your conclusion.

- Freewriting

  > Freewrite for 10 minutes about what you might include in your conclusion. Don't worry about grammar, punctuation, or having fully formed ideas. The point of freewriting is to discover ideas.

  > Think about how you can articulate, or express, the significance of your topic in the conclusion.

  > Rephrase your main idea to show the depth of your knowledge and support for the information you presented.

  > Write your conclusion.

↻ YOUR TURN

Choose the best answer to each question.

1. Which of the following elements belongs in a concluding paragraph?

   ○ A. a statement that rephrases the thesis
   ○ B. reasons and relevant evidence to support a claim
   ○ C. transitions to link major sections of a text
   ○ D. a "hook" and the first appearance of the thesis statement containing a claim

2. Below is Alex's conclusion from another draft. What is one piece of information that Alex needs to include as he continues to revise?

> When writers make a declaration that challenges the status quo, they put their reputations on the line. They make themselves a target for ridicule and risk alienation. The Supreme Court knew the implications of their verdict, but they did it anyways. Likewise, George Marshall was well aware of the fact that his speech about rebuilding Europe—especially Germany—might be met with resistance, but he continued to move forward with his plans, garnering national attention and international assistance.

   ○ A. Alex neglects to support his ideas with relevant evidence.
   ○ B. Alex neglects to discuss both of the texts that he has selected.
   ○ C. Alex needs to discuss other texts besides the two mentioned in his essay.
   ○ D. Alex needs to explain how these courageous actions connect to the idea of winning.

✏ WRITE

Use the checklist to revise the conclusion of your argumentative essay.

Argumentative Writing Process: Revise

| PLAN | DRAFT | REVISE | EDIT AND PUBLISH |

You have written a draft of your argumentative essay. You have also received input from your peers about how to improve it. Now you are going to revise your draft.

◀◀ REVISION GUIDE

Examine your draft to find areas for revision. Keep in mind your purpose and audience as you revise for clarity, development, organization, and style. Use the guide below to help you review:

Review	Revise	Example
Clarity		
Identify all pronouns, and determine if it is clear to whom you are referring.	Use the authors' or individuals' names to identify whom you are talking about.	Instead, it takes the combined effort of focused leaders like ~~these~~ George Marshall and the members of the Supreme Court to rally others around their vision for progress.

Review	Revise	Example
Development		
Identify the textual evidence that supports your claims as well as places where you have included commentary. Annotate places where you feel there is not enough textual evidence to support your ideas or where you have failed to provide commentary.	Focus on a single idea or claim, and add your personal reflections in the form of commentary or add support in the form of textual evidence.	Marshall charges his audience to continue the war, stating that the United States has a "vast responsibility which history has clearly placed upon our country." With financial assistance from the United States, Europe can re-emerge from devastation. The use of an emotional appeal throughout the speech reminds the audience that the United States is uniquely positioned to champion the rise of free and democratic nations.
Organization		
Review your body paragraphs. Are they coherent? Identify and annotate any sentences within and across paragraphs that don't flow in a clear and logical way.	Rewrite the sentences so they are clear and flow logically.	The children and families who risked their lives to go to school and the lawyers who stuck with the case combined their efforts in defense of African Americans' access to education and, more broadly, their civil rights. ~~In 1952, the justices unanimously ruled that segregation in schools was unconstitutional.~~ The case made it to the Supreme Court of the United States, and in 1952 the justices unanimously ruled that segregation in schools was unconstitutional. Chief Justice Warren opens the decision by stating, "we cannot turn the clocks back" and "We must consider public education in the light of its full development and its present place in America."

Review	Revise	Example
Style: Word Choice		
Identify any weak adjectives, nouns, or verbs.	Replace weak adjectives, nouns, or verbs with strong, descriptive, and precise language.	Although Americans may be ~~tired~~ weary from war, the fight must continue. Marshall charges his audience to continue the war, stating that the United States has a "vast responsibility which history has clearly placed upon our country." With financial assistance from the United States, Europe can ~~come out~~ re-emerge from devastation.
Style: Sentence Fluency		
Read aloud your writing and listen to the way the text sounds. Does it sound choppy? Or does it flow smoothly with rhythm, movement, and emphasis on important details and events?	Rewrite a key passage, making your sentences longer or shorter to achieve a better flow of writing and the effect you want your reader to feel.	Here, the author is laying out the purpose for delivering his speech. ~~He argues that~~: Although the United States and its allies have sacrificed much to win the war, peace cannot be ensured while Europe is on the brink of chaos. Marshall makes a stirring case for the United States to aid their former enemies. ~~He,~~ and he starts by showing just how high the stakes are for Europe and the world.

✏ WRITE

Use the revision guide, as well as your peer reviews, to help you evaluate your argumentative essay to determine areas that should be revised.

Skill: Style

••• CHECKLIST FOR STYLE

First, reread the draft of your argumentative essay and identify the following:

- slang, colloquialisms, contractions, abbreviations, or a conversational tone
- places where you could use academic language in order to help persuade your readers
- the use of the first person (*I*) or the second person (*you*)
- statements that express judgment or emotion, rather than objective statements that rely on facts and evidence
- places where you could vary sentence structure and length by using compound, complex, and compound-complex sentences

  > for guidance on effective ways of varying syntax, use a style guide

- incorrect uses of the conventions of standard English for grammar, spelling, capitalization, and punctuation

Establish and maintain a formal style in your essay, using the following questions as a guide:

- Have I avoided slang in favor of academic language?
- Did I consistently use a third-person perspective, using third-person pronouns (*he, she, they*)?
- Have I maintained an objective tone without expressing my own judgments and emotions?
- Have I used varied sentence lengths and different sentence structures? Did I consider using style guides to learn about effective ways of varying syntax?

  > Where should I make some sentences longer by using conjunctions to connect independent clauses, dependent clauses, and phrases?

  > Where should I make some sentences shorter by separating independent clauses?

- Have I correctly used the conventions of standard English?

YOUR TURN

Choose the best answer to each question.

1. Which type of stylistic error did Alex make in this line from a previous draft?

> I think Marshall was a very strong person and he gives me hope.

- ○ A. Alex's use of capitalization is incorrect.
- ○ B. The sentence is too complex.
- ○ C. Alex uses the pronouns *I* and *me* and makes a statement based on his feelings.
- ○ D. Alex uses slang.

2. Below are two sentences from a previous draft of Alex's essay. How should these sentences be rewritten to address possible stylistic errors?

> The use of a series of emotional appeals throughout the speech challenges the complacency of allies who think the war is finished. And it also encourages listeners to really think hard about the decision at hand.

- ○ A. The use of a series of emotional appeals throughout the speech challenges the complacency of allies who think the war is finished and I think it encourages listeners to think critically about the decision at hand.
- ○ B. The use of a series of emotional appeals throughout the speech challenges the complacency of allies who think the war is finished encourages listeners to think critically about the decision at hand.
- ○ C. The use of a series of emotional appeals throughout the speech challenges the complacency of allies who think the war is finished and encourages listeners to think critically about the decision at hand.
- ○ D. These sentences should not be changed.

WRITE

Use the checklist to revise a paragraph of your argumentative essay to improve the style.

Grammar: Sentence Fragments

A sentence fragment is a group of words that lacks a subject, a predicate, or both. A fragment does not express a complete thought.

Every sentence must have a subject and a predicate to express a complete thought. The subject part of a sentence names whom or what the sentence is about. The predicate part tells what the subject does or has. It can also describe what the subject is or is like.

Term	Definition	Example
complete sentence	contains a subject and a predicate to express a complete thought	He objected to the T-shirt logo, calling it disgusting and vulgar. Catch the Moon
sentence fragment	a group of words that lacks a subject, a predicate, or both	Not too far. Call It Sleep

⟳ YOUR TURN

1. What change is needed to form a complete sentence?

> Barked continually from midnight until 4:00 A.M.

- ○ A. Add the subject: *My neighbor's dog.*
- ○ B. Remove the words **from midnight.**
- ○ C. Change **continually** to *constantly.*
- ○ D. No change needs to be made.

2. What change is needed to form a complete sentence?

> My older sister Becky, who had twins at the beginning of January.

- ○ A. Add *healthy* before **twins.**
- ○ B. Add the conjunction *but* after **twins.**
- ○ C. Add the predicate: *decided to work from home.*
- ○ D. No change needs to be made.

3. What change is needed to form a complete sentence?

> No one but Marella was in the car when the accident occurred.

- ○ A. Add a detail about whose car it was.
- ○ B. Add a colon after **Marella.**
- ○ C. Remove the phrase **in the car.**
- ○ D. No change needs to be made.

4. What change is needed to form a complete sentence?

> Walked along Sixth Street, looked up, and saw a hot-air balloon.

- ○ A. Before **walked,** add the subject: *My friends and I.*
- ○ B. Replace the period with a question mark.
- ○ C. Add *Wandered and* in front of **walked.**
- ○ D. No change needs to be made.

Grammar: Run-On Sentences

A run-on sentence is two or more sentences incorrectly written as one sentence. Correct a run-on sentence by doing one of the following:

- Change the independent clauses into two separate sentences with a period after each
- Separate the independent clauses with a semicolon (;)
- Separate the independent clauses with a comma and a coordinating conjunction (*and, or, but*)
- Separate the independent clauses with a subordinating conjunction (*because, although,* etc.)
- Separate the independent clauses with a semicolon or period and then add a conjunctive adverb followed by a comma (*however, finally, therefore,* etc.)

Run-On Sentence	Strategy	Text
Scot has arrived, and brings news that he expected to find all peace and Quietness here as he left them at home, you will have more particulars than I am able to send you, from much better hands.	Add a period to separate the independent clauses into two separate sentences.	Scot has arrived, and brings news that he expected to find all peace and Quietness here as he left them at home. You will have more particulars than I am able to send you, from much better hands. Letters to John Adams
They walked through the diningroom where the firebrick in the hearth was as yellow as the day it was laid, his mother could not bear to see it blackened.	Remove the comma and add a subordinating conjunction.	They walked through the diningroom where the firebrick in the hearth was as yellow as the day it was laid because his mother could not bear to see it blackened. The Road

⟳ YOUR TURN

1. How should this sentence be changed?

> It is smaller than the crane it has a longer neck.

- ○ A. Add a comma after **crane**.
- ○ B. Add a comma and *but* after **crane**.
- ○ C. Put a period after **crane**.
- ○ D. No change needs to be made to this sentence.

2. How should this sentence be changed?

> My aunt Debra owns three dogs she wants to get another one.

- ○ A. Add a comma after **dogs**.
- ○ B. Add *big* before **dogs**.
- ○ C. Add a comma and the word *but* after **dogs**.
- ○ D. No change needs to be made to this sentence.

3. How should this sentence be changed?

> My jeans were hanging on the clothesline, and a wren tried to build a nest in them.

- ○ A. Replace **and** with *therefore*.
- ○ B. Delete the word **and**.
- ○ C. Change the comma to a semicolon.
- ○ D. No change needs to be made to this sentence.

4. How should this sentence be changed?

> Sharon brought cheesecake to the class reunion Marla brought brownies.

- ○ A. Add a comma after **reunion**.
- ○ B. Add a comma and the word *and* after **reunion**.
- ○ C. Add a semicolon and the word *and* after **reunion**.
- ○ D. No change needs to be made to this sentence.

Please note that excerpts and passages in the StudySync® library and this workbook are intended as touchstones to generate interest in an author's work. The excerpts and passages do not substitute for the reading of entire texts, and StudySync® strongly recommends that students seek out and purchase the whole literary or informational work in order to experience it as the author intended. Links to online resellers are available in our digital library. In addition, complete works may be ordered through an authorized reseller by filling out and returning to StudySync® the order form enclosed in this workbook.

Reading & Writing Companion   **149**

Grammar: Parallel Structure

Parallel structure, or parallelism, is a deliberate repetition of words, phrases, or other grammatical structures to achieve an effect. Parallel structure creates a pattern to show that two or more ideas have equal weight in a sentence. Words, phrases, or clauses joined by a conjunction should be parallel within a sentence. Using parallel structure also helps writers clarify their ideas and avoid extra unnecessary language. Read below to learn more about situations in which writers often use parallel structure.

Strategy	Not Parallel	Parallel
Use parallel structure when listing elements.	Some common gases are colorless, odorless, and **they won't hurt you.**	Some common gases are colorless, odorless, and **harmless.**
Use parallel structure when using correlative conjunctions. Correlative conjunctions are used in pairs and include the following: — either/or — neither/nor — not only/but also — both/and	The waterfall not only looked beautiful but also **was making a soothing sound.**	The waterfall not only looked beautiful but also **sounded soothing.**
Use parallel structure when comparing elements.	Running is just as effective exercise as **when you ride a bike.**	Running is just as effective exercise as **riding a bike.**
Use parallel structure when using the gerund, or -*ing*, form of words.	James enjoys outdoor activities such as hiking, camping, and **to play tennis.**	James enjoys outdoor activities such as hiking, camping, and **playing tennis.**
Use parallel structure with infinitive phrases, or verbs preceded by the word *to*. Note that it is necessary to write *to* only before the first infinitive, not before each one.	Thom liked to read the paper, cut out articles, and **taping** them to the wall.	Thom liked to read the paper, cut out articles, and **tape** them to the wall.

⟳ YOUR TURN

1. How should this sentence be changed?

> Traveling over the winter holidays can be difficult because the airports are crowded, the lines are long, and bad weather.

- ○ A. Replace **the airports are crowded** with **crowded airports.**
- ○ B. Replace **bad weather** with **the weather is bad.**
- ○ C. Replace **the lines are long** with **long lines.**
- ○ D. No change needs to be made to this sentence.

2. How should this sentence be changed?

> The campers had to dive off the dock, swim across the lake, and paddle back in a canoe.

- ○ A. Insert **to** before **swim.**
- ○ B. Insert **to** before **paddle.**
- ○ C. Replace **to dive** with **diving.**
- ○ D. No change needs to be made to this sentence.

3. How should this sentence be changed?

> William looked behind the door, in the closet, and checked under the bed, but he could not find his other sneaker.

- ○ A. Delete **checked.**
- ○ B. Replace **looked** with **is looking.**
- ○ C. Insert **still** after **he.**
- ○ D. No change needs to be made to this sentence.

4. How should this sentence be changed?

> Mom's morning routine is to make coffee, read the paper, and getting dressed for work.

- ○ A. Replace **to make** with **making.**
- ○ B. Replace **read** with **reading.**
- ○ C. Replace **getting** with **get.**
- ○ D. No change needs to be made to this sentence.

Please note that excerpts and passages in the StudySync® library and this workbook are intended as touchstones to generate interest in an author's work. The excerpts and passages do not substitute for the reading of entire texts, and StudySync® strongly recommends that students seek out and purchase the whole literary or informational work in order to experience it as the author intended. Links to online resellers are available in our digital library. In addition, complete works may be ordered through an authorized reseller by filling out and returning to StudySync® the order form enclosed in this workbook.

Reading & Writing Companion   151

Argumentative Writing Process: Edit and Publish

PLAN	DRAFT	REVISE	EDIT AND PUBLISH

You have revised your argumentative essay based on your peer feedback and your own examination.

Now, it is time to edit your argumentative essay. When you revised, you focused on the content of your argumentative essay. You probably looked at your essay's clarity and development. When you edit, you focus on the mechanics of your essay, paying close attention to things like grammar and punctuation.

Use the checklist below to guide you as you edit:

☐ Does each sentence express a complete thought?

☐ Have I properly structured sentences with more than one independent clause?

☐ Have I used parallel structure properly?

☐ Have I spelled everything correctly?

Notice some edits Alex has made:

- Corrected a spelling mistake
- Changed a verb form to create parallelism
- Added a verb to correct a sentence fragment

George Marshall also uses the power of words to inspire change. Unlike the United States Supreme Court ~~justisses~~ justices who rely on the clarity of their reasoning to make a point, Marshall uses an emotional appeal to generate meaning, make a point, and ~~persuades~~ persuade his audience in his speech about rebuilding Europe after World War II. Marshall, who was appointed to the position of Secretary of State by President Truman, delivered a commencement address at Harvard University after the Paris Peace Treaties were signed in 1947. In the speech's first sentences, Marshall says, "the world situation is very serious." Here, the author is laying out the purpose for delivering his speech.

✏ WRITE

Use the questions in the checklist, as well as your peer reviews, to help you evaluate your argumentative essay to determine places that need editing. Then, edit your essay to correct those errors.

Once you have made all your corrections, you are ready to publish your work. You can distribute your writing to family and friends, hang it on a bulletin board, or post it on your blog. If you publish online, share the link with your family, friends, and classmates.

Please note that excerpts and passages in the StudySync® library and this workbook are intended as touchstones to generate interest in an author's work. The excerpts and passages do not substitute for the reading of entire texts, and StudySync® strongly recommends that students seek out and purchase the whole literary or informational work in order to experience it as the author intended. Links to online resellers are available in our digital library. In addition, complete works may be ordered through an authorized reseller by filling out and returning to StudySync® the order form enclosed in this workbook.

Reading & Writing Companion   153

PHOTO/IMAGE CREDITS:

cover, iStock.com/scanrail
p. iii, iStock.com/DNY59
p. ix, iStock.com/scanrail
p. x, Lorraine Hansberry - BTJP1G, Everett Collection Inc/Alamy Stock Photo
p. x, John Hersey - Everett Collection Historical/Alamy Stock Photo
p. x, Langston Hughes - Underwood Archives/Contributor/Archive Photos/Getty Images
p. x, Jack Kerouac -Bettmann/Contributor/Getty
p. x, Martin Luther King Jr. - Bettmann/Contributor/Bettmann/Getty Images
p. xi, George Marshall - Culture Club/Contributor/Hulton Archive/Getty
p. xi, Arthur Miller - Bettmann/Contributor/Bettmann/Getty
p. xi, Aimee Nezhukumatahil - Used by permission of Aimee Nezhukumatathil.
p. xi, Flannery O'Connor - Apic/RETIRED/Contributor/Hulton Archive/Getty
p. xii, iStock.com/Pgiam
p. 2, Hulton Deutsch/Corbis Historical/Getty Images
p. 3, George Skadding/The LIFE Picture Collection/Getty Images
p. 4, Bettman/Bettman/Getty Images
p. 7, iStock.com/Pgiam
p. 8, iSock.com/RichLegg
p. 12, iStock.com/Anton_Sokolov
p. 28, iStock.com/Anton_Sokolov
p. 29, iStock.com/ValentinaPhotos
p. 30, iStock.com/ValentinaPhotos
p. 32, iStock.com/Orla
p. 33, iStock.com/Orla
p. 34, iStock.com/Anton_Sokolov
p. 35, ©iStock.com/kieferpix
p. 36, TASS/TASS/Getty Images
p. 37, Hulton Deutsch/Corbis Historical/Getty Images
p. 41, ©iStock.com/kieferpix
p. 42, iStock.com/Brostock
p. 43, iStock.com/Brostock
p. 44, iStock.com/Caval
p. 45, iStock.com/Caval
p. 47, iStock.com/Murat Göçmen
p. 48, iStock.com/Murat Göçmen
p. 49, iStock.com/kieferpix
p. 50, iStock.com/Marius_Kempf
p. 54, iStock.com/alexeys
p. 57, iStock.com/poco_bw
p. 61, iStock.com/poco_bw
p. 62, iStock/Spanishalex

p. 63, iStock/Spanishalex
p. 64, iStock.com/Dominique_Lavoie
p. 65, iStock.com/Dominique_Lavoie
p. 66, iStock.com/poco_bw
p. 67, Matthew Abbott/Contributor/Moment/GettyImages
p. 68, Everett Collection Inc/Alamy Stock Photo
p. 71, UtCon Collection/Alamy Stock Photo
p. 73, Matthew Abbott/Contributor/Moment/GettyImages
p. 74, iStock.com/
p. 77, iStock.com/PeopleImages
p. 80, iStock.com/franny-anne
p. 81, Bettmann/Bettmann/Getty Images
p. 83, iStock.com/franny-anne
p. 84, iStock.com/peepo
p. 85, iStock.com/peepo
p. 86, iStock.com/Orla
p. 87, iStock.com/Orla
p. 88, iStock.com/janrysavy
p. 89, iStock.com/janrysavy
p. 90, iStock.com/franny-anne
p. 91, iStock.com/SonerCdem
p. 92, Boston Globe/Boston Globe/Getty Images
p. 95, iStock.com/Michael Warren
p. 105, iStock.com/Michael Warren
p. 106, iStock.com/ThomasVogel
p. 107, iStock.com/ThomasVogel
p. 108, iStock.com/pixhook
p. 109, iStock.com/pixhook
p. 110, iStock.com/antoni_halim
p. 111, iStock.com/antoni_halim
p. 112, iStock.com/Michael Warren
p. 113, iStock.com/hanibaram, iStock.com/seb_ra, iStock.com/Martin Barraud
p. 114, iStock.com/Martin Barraud
p. 122, iStock.com/gopixa
p. 124, iStock.com/fstop123
p. 127, iStock.com/Domin_domin
p. 129, iStock.com/Martin Barraud
p. 135, iStock.com/bo1982
p. 137, iStock.com/Jeff_Hu
p. 139, iStock.com/stevedangers
p. 141, iStock.com/Martin Barraud
p. 144, iStock.com/Fodor90
p. 146, ©iStock.com/wildpixel
p. 148, ©iStock.com/wildpixel
p. 150, iStock/Vimvertigo
p. 152, iStock.com/Martin Barraud

studysync®

Text Fulfillment Through StudySync

If you are interested in specific titles, please fill out the form below and we will check availability through our partners.

ORDER DETAILS

Date:

TITLE	AUTHOR	Paperback/ Hardcover	Specific Edition *If Applicable*	Quantity

SHIPPING INFORMATION

Contact:

Title:

School/District:

Address Line 1:

Address Line 2:

Zip or Postal Code:

Phone:

Mobile:

Email:

BILLING INFORMATION ☐ *SAME AS SHIPPING*

Contact:

Title:

School/District:

Address Line 1:

Address Line 2:

Zip or Postal Code:

Phone:

Mobile:

Email:

PAYMENT INFORMATION

☐ CREDIT CARD

Name on Card:

Card Number:　　　　　　Expiration Date:　　　　　Security Code:

☐ PO

Purchase Order Number:

StudySync Text Fulfillment, BookheadEd Learning, LLC
610 Daniel Young Drive | Sonoma, CA 95476